The Adventures Of A

FREE LUNCH JUNKIE

EARL BRONSTEEN

About the Author

Earl Bronsteen is an eighty-five-year-young Brooklyn-born, Manhattan-raised, Yale-educated (sociology major, varsity basketball minor), CPA, business executive turned photographer turned installation and conceptual artist turned author who has his sights next set on a trek up Mount Everest, if time and weather permit.

His first book, *Contemporary Art Appreciation 101*, is a best seller in the arcane world of artists' books. This limited edition, 304-page tome satire is embellished with objects of every kind and description, including an air freshener, gum, music, aromatic postal stamps, and much, much more.

Leading public and private libraries including The New York Public Library, The Library of Congress, the British Library, Yale, Dartmouth, UCLA and many more, have purchased the book.

Photo by Peter Bronsteen

Earl at his desk assembling *Contemporary Art Appreciation 101*.

DEDICATION

I dedicate this book to Judy, my loving wife of forty-four years. It seems like only yesterday that I picked her up at the pool at the Americana Hotel in Puerto Rico, where we were both vacationing. Little did I realize that day that she would become my muse, editor, and staunchest booster in my artistic and writing endeavors. Like a fine wine, she improves with age.

ACKNOWLEDGEMENTS

This book would not have been possible without the committed efforts and wholehearted support of:

Richard, Peter, and Bill, my three sons, and their wives, Donna, Alissa, and Tanya, who from the very beginning encouraged me to write this book.

Alan Cohen, my erudite and unpaid literary adviser. His painstaking editing uncovered numerous typos and grammatical errors just before I was ready to go to press. If you find any errors blame him not me. Alan's constructive suggestions were incorporated into the final version.

Sylvia and Stan Teitelbaum, longtime friends. They spent part of their vacation reading a draft of this book, and we spent hours going over their suggestions.

Tim Reilly and Phil Stevenson, whose advice was invaluable.

Bill Sarnoff, who extended himself on my behalf.

And last, but certainly not least, my oncologists, Dr. Andrew Zelenetz and Dr. Harold Richter, who've kept me going these past twenty years.

TABLE OF CONTENTS

MY ADVENTURES AS A FREE LUNCH SEMINAR JUNKIE

The phone rang, jarring me out of my afternoon nap. I stumbled out of bed and lifted the receiver to my ear. "Hello, Mr. Bronsteen, I'm calling to let you know that we must cancel our free lunch seminar scheduled for 11:30 a.m. tomorrow because our speaker has suddenly taken ill."

I put the phone down and slumped dejectedly at my desk. What an inauspicious start to the research on my new project.

But I've put the dessert before the appetizer. Let me explain.

A few months ago I completed my first attempt at writing a "best seller"—"All My Ancestors," a fictional story about an immigrant family in the 1890s. I sent a synopsis to seventy-five literary agents seeking representation. Their unanimous lack of interest was disheartening.

I went into a deep funk. Months of hard work went down the drain, and I decided not to write again. (Seventy-five literary agents breathed a sigh of relief.)

What was I to do with the balance of my "Arthritic Golden Years"? After months of unproductive agonizing, I became an intellectual sloth finding solace only in my two naps a day.

Then one morning an ad in the local newspaper caught my eye. It touted a seminar on reverse mortgages, followed by a *free* lunch at a very fine restaurant. I have a reputation for being cheap, and whether this description is true or not, the words *free lunch* resonated through my being. I decided to kill three birds with one stone.

One, I'd write a story about the numerous free lunch seminars offered in South Florida,

Two, I'd get my ass out of the house, and…

Three, I'd save a few bucks.

That should explain my disappointment upon receiving the phone call I told you about in the first paragraph. But as you'll read in the pages that follow, my luck changed; and in the ensuing months, I was able to eat my way through a swathe of South Florida's finest restaurants without so much as forking up a dime.

THE FOLLOWING EPISDES TOOK PLACE BETWEEN

11:30 A.M. ON MAY 25, 2010 AND

12:00 P.M. ON FEBRUARY 11, 2011

MY FIRST FREE LUNCH SEMINAR

When I received a mailer for a "Seminar & Free Luncheon" at The Cheesecake Factory right here in Boca Raton, I had dreams of "Fried chicken served over mashed potatoes slathered with fresh, creamery butter, plus shortcake biscuits, covered with country gravy, topped off with a large slice of their famous cheesecake for dessert."

Memories of my last meal years ago at The Cheesecake Factory danced in my mind, a mega-thousand-calorie, artery-clogging feast. I devoured that sumptuous repast in the days before I started to pay attention to my diet, and I have never gone back.

I tore open the mailer to read about the seminar titled "Straight Talk About Reverse Mortgages." With my cholesterol now a not-too-shabby 195, and my HDLs way above the bad ones, I felt no guilt as I quickly called the number on the invitation and made an appointment for my first seminar.

I surmised that I could put up with an hour spiel about any kind of mortgage (reverse, adverse, or perverse) just to be able to dig my teeth into one of those glistening, fried chicken thighs; at my age one glistening thigh is pretty much the same as another glistening thigh.

I invited a friend (Herb) to join me as my guest, figuring to kill two more birds with the same stone. I'd enjoy a free meal, and for sure Herb would feel obligated to reciprocate and treat me to lunch.

Here's a transcript of the notes I took at the seminar:

11:30 a.m. Arrive at the appointed time and follow the signs to a back room, where eight tables are set up for groups of four. Herb and I take seats at a back table and survey the rather plain room populated with about twenty rather plain seniors.

Waitress takes our (soft) drink order, and we examine the special lunch menu. There are fourteen choices, but no fried chicken, no biscuits, and no mashed potatoes. And no dessert. Look up at the moderator. He smiles back at me. Swear he looks just like "The Grinch Who Stole Christmas."

Order what guesstimate to be the most expensive entrée, a Factory Chopped Salad: "A delicious blend of Chopped Romaine, Grilled Chicken, Tomato, Avocado, Corn, Bacon, Blue Cheese, and Apple with Vinaigrette Dressing."

11:45 a.m. The Grinch launches into his sales pitch. I quietly signal for a refill of my iced tea. He finishes forty minutes later and opens the floor to questions. Don't want him to think I just came for the free lunch, so ask a question. He seems pleased.

My salad is delicious. Herb asks the waitress for bread. Can see he is getting into the spirit of things. No one else has bread. One single woman orders cheesecake for dessert a la carte. Must have inherited a bundle. Probably lives high up in a penthouse condo facing the ocean.

Then the Grinch walks up to each person with an appointment book in hand and tries to arrange private meetings at each participant's home. The crux of the whole seminar is encapsulated in these next few minutes. When he gets to our table, the pressure in the room is palpable. My friend and I say we want to think about it. The Grinch halfheartedly fights back a sneer. "I'll call in a week," he promises.

Try to gauge how many of my fellow attendees are freeloaders. The "sport" who ordered cheesecake certainly wasn't here for a free chicken thigh. Am surprised how many people sign up for a follow-up visit. Once this man gets inside a potential customer's living room, their goose is cooked; their home is reverse-mortgaged.

PS. Sure enough, a week later the Grinch called to try to arrange an appointment. In the meantime I had gone online to get further information about reverse mortgages. My research revealed that the Grinch had not been fully forthcoming in his sales presentation about some of the intricacies of the program. But my overall impression was that for some seniors, these mortgages made sense, but not for me. Even after he agreed that this program was not the right one for me, he stayed on the phone for almost half an hour trying to convince me to set up a home visit. He was as tenacious as a bulldog, but I'm no pussycat.

PPS. As of this writing, my guest, Herb, has not seen fit to reciprocate, but I haven't given up—common courtesy isn't dead yet in Boca.

Dollars and Cents Recap: I figured I saved about $15 with my Cheesecake Factory Chopped Salad and beverage, less about $2 for gas. Fortunately, the parking lot was empty, so I didn't have to tip for valet parking.

BONEHEAD MEETS BONEFISH

My second luncheon seminar got off to a rather inauspicious start, and things went from bad to worse. I waved good-bye to my wife, Judy, and headed out the door on the way to my early-dinner seminar in Boynton Beach. "You're not going dressed like that, are you?" Judy gasped as she stared at my unpressed khaki shorts, ~~unkempt~~ half-kempt polo shirt, and white tennis socks.

My first reaction to her words was, "They're playing our song," because I've heard that refrain so many times before in our forty-plus years of wedded bliss. "I'm just going to a free dinner seminar at Bonefish Grill, and the invitation didn't say anything about the dress code," I retorted. Since Judy wasn't accompanying me, she couldn't threaten, "Unless you change your pants, I'm not going," so I blew her a kiss and headed off to meet my fellow seminar attendees.

It took twenty-five minutes to get to Boynton Beach and find Bonefish Grill. I arrived just at 4:00 p.m. When I entered the empty restaurant, I spied a group of about twenty people at one end of the room seated in two rows in front of a projector screen, listening to a man with a pointer in his hand. Two stern-faced ladies near the door stopped me and asked what I wanted. When I told them that I was there for the seminar, they told me that it had started at 3:00 p.m. and that it was almost over. They gave me that look that younger people often give to a senior citizen who they are sure is Alzheimered.

I was chagrined at having gotten the time wrong. I felt even worse because I had checked the appointment in my daily calendar that very morning, but for some reason I had confused the 3:00 p.m. starting time with the 4:00 p. m. dinnertime. I tried to redeem myself with the two women by saying, "What a pretty kettle of fish," but their faces were set in stone.

I had an urge to ask them if I could go in and see what the men who were attending the seminar were wearing, but suppressed it. I wanted to wait around and see what they were serving for dinner. I tried to edge closer, but was cut off at the pass by the two women gatekeepers who were spitting images of Scylla and Charybdis. (In Greek mythology Scylla was a creature who was rooted to one spot in the ocean and regularly ate sailors who passed by too closely. Charybdis was depicted with a single gaping mouth that sucked in huge quantities of water and belched them out three times a day, creating whirlpools.) It was them all right.

I turned my car around and headed back to Boca with my tail between my legs. At least I hadn't heeded Judy's admonition and bothered to change my clothes. From what I could see of the guests at the seminar, a personal shopper at K-Mart dressed them.

I arrived home before five. Judy was surprised to see me return so soon and asked what had happened. I decided to make her day and answered, "The sponsor said I wasn't dressed appropriately and sent me away." She gave me a quizzical look, desperately wanting to believe my story, but knowing it wasn't true. I had scrambled eggs for dinner…better than humble pie.

BONEFISH GRILL REDUX

Seven days after my embarrassing gaffe—when I arrived at Bonefish Grill and was turned away from the seminar because I was an hour late—I'm back in Boynton Beach for my 3:00 p.m. seminar and 4:00 p.m. free dinner. Talk about early bird dinners. I ate an early light lunch at home. I hoped our host would serve Dover Sole (boned at the table, *s'il vous plait*).

2:40 p.m. Arrive twenty minutes early at restaurant just to be sure. Receptionist tells me I came too early and to have a seat in the bar. Tempted to ask if she has eaten any sailors recently, but demur.

2:45 p.m. All clear. Other receptionist asks for my name and photo ID. Never told would need ID. Pull out my driver's license. She says I look familiar. Reply in a low voice that I had shown up an hour late at last week's seminar. She remembers. Smirks.

Shown to a table set for ten and seated next to a group of three women. Minutes later sour-faced receptionist accosts one of the women, saying she doesn't resemble the photo on the ID she had presented. Woman protests that it's a bad photo but that it's hers. Receptionist is wary, not so sure. Then relents and explains to group that she only did this because they get many people who try to come back time after time for the free dinner. Good sign. Meal must be delicious.

Open napkin to find knife, fork, and spoon. Another good sign. No cookie for dessert here. Banana split goes well with fish and meat. Table fills up with three couples, two of whom are pretty old (my age), plus the three women. I'm dressed as casually as everyone else. I'd like to get a group photo to show Judy, but afraid this will blow my cover.

Menu on table lists salad, choice of chicken marsala or tilapia with choice of two sauces, plus choice of beverage. Instructed to circle our choices. Chose the fish and iced tea.

Man opposite me leans toward wife and asks what he had for dinner last night. She says fish. He can't decide what to order. Waitress has collected everyone else's choices. Man tells her he can't decide what to have. She looks at him as if he has just arrived from Mars. Tells him there are only two choices. Says testily, "Do you want chicken or fish?" He mutters, "Chicken." She asks, "Do you want iced tea, soda, or water?" Soda it is. She fills in his menu choices and heads off in a huff to the kitchen. Exasperated server has had it up to here with seniors.

Each table setting has an INFO Sheet, and we are told to fill it out with our name, address, etc., and check off the subjects we are interested in (annuities, taxes, bonds). There's a box to check telling what day of week and time is best for "Free Complimentary Appointment & Financial Analysis." Man opposite whispers to his wife, "Free" and smiles. He's not as addled as waitress supposes.

3:00 p.m. Nondescript speaker introduces himself. Recounts his experience and relates that his firm offers investments, annuities, taxes, long term health plan, bonds, and much more. I wouldn't call him a silver-tongued orator—more of a brass-tongued barker. He points to a flip chart on a stand, which he refers to frequently during the hour. Starts song and dance. Speaker likes to ask questions of the audience to keep them involved and awake, not necessarily in that order. Only problem is that he's talking about the Federal Reserve, interest rate policy, and the like, and this group is financially challenged. Embarrassing pause after he asks a simple question of the group. I keep quiet. Finally one woman blurts out an outrageous answer that almost takes the speaker's breath away. He can hardly contain himself. Tries easier and easier questions, but never finds our level.

Talks about investments. Mentions two popular stocks that he says will be 20–40 percent higher by year-end and sevenfold higher in five years. People perk up. Man asks, "What about gold?" Speaker answers, "No one has ever made money investing in gold!" Audience gasps. He reiterates and then gives a ridiculous explanation of why. I realize that he's not too much more financially sophisticated than his audience. I notice that his feet are quite small. I guess that's why they fit so easily in his mouth.

Speaker said Federal Reserve has nothing to do with interest rates; only a war raises interest rates. Says, "Warren Buffet never sold a stock." (More gasps.) Man tries to make speaker eat his own words by asserting The New York Times said, "Buffet just sold Kraft." Speaker replies through gritted teeth, "No, he didn't."

4:00 p.m. Its been a trying hour for the speaker and for the audience (but not as bad as it was for the tilapia, who gave up his life so there'd be this seminar). The speaker never talked about the subjects the guests were interested in, and he felt as if he had been talking to a bunch of knuckleheads. Speaker ends by going up to each person to set up "Free Complimentary Appointment" in his office. A few try to duck, but he pressures them to pick a date, and if they can't make it, they can change it. I pick a Wednesday morning and get an appointment card reminder. A few guests ask questions that he doesn't answer. Wonder if he knows the answer, but doesn't want to give it out before the Complimentary Appointment, or if he just doesn't know. My instincts lean toward the latter.

4:05 p.m. Waitresses bring in salad, followed by entrée, bread, and beverage. No one seems to think it's strange we're eating dinner so early, and the food flies into our mouths. Delicious dinner, all agree. Two couples tell about different restaurants where they have good two-for-one meals. Copy names down.

4:30 p.m. Bid adieu to my dinner companions and head back to Boca.

Summary: This restaurant had the best food of any of the seminars so far, but I will leave no stone unturned until I find the Holy Grail of the free lunch circuit: steak. On the way out I picked up a menu from the restaurant—the tilapia cost $14.90, salad $1.50, and tea $2.50. I don't think I made much of a profit because I had to drive thirty miles each day, but I can see why a sophisticated freeloader would be willing to put up with a boring one-hour lecture to try to sneak back for this early, early bird dinner. Maybe in a few months I'll try again, but I'm afraid the receptionist might recognize me. I'll wear a suit and tie as a disguise, but not a sailor suit.

PS. Many months later I noticed another series of seminars advertised by this same firm. I was astounded to see one new wrinkle in the ad. It read, "A $400 charge to investment sales representatives or financial advisers." (Sounds like a "wool pullover" to me—"I wonder whose eye's he's trying to pull the wool over")

DRESS CODE: BUSINESS CASUAL

You can imagine my surprise when I received a call at 8 o'clock one evening in June to confirm my appointment for the next day's seminar. It wasn't the lateness of the call but the fact that the caller told me that the dress code for tomorrow's event was "business casual." I couldn't figure out why the company that was forking up the dough for my lunch cared what I wore. I wondered if my wife had called the sponsors and told them that I was planning to wear shorts and that they should "head me off at the pass."

The stern voice also told me to bring a business card (which I don't have anymore) and a picture ID. I wondered if I had signed up for a clandestine seminar on how to become a member of the CIA, but I doubt that the CIA would give a free lunch in today's tough economic climate. I wondered if the CIA ever considered sponsoring a free lunch seminar in Afghanistan offering tips on money laundering, hoping to ensnare a few gullible Taliban. If they did, I bet they'd serve a dish with poppy seeds. But I digress, back to reality.

I had second thoughts about going to the seminar, but since the sponsor was also giving away an MP3 player, I figured I'd take a chance. I don't know what an MP3 player is, but free is free, and with all this professionalism I'm sure lunch will be scrumptious.

11:35 p.m. Arrive at Embassy Suites Hotel in Boca Raton and follow signs to "Internet Marketing Conference." Check in at desk and affix nametag (Earl) to my shirt. Receive coupon for free MP3 player.

Enter large meeting room and told to take any seat in the first three rows. There are about nine rows of tables with chairs set up facing the screen in front. Each row has about seventeen seats. Nine times seventeen equals 153. Must expect a big crowd.

11:40 a.m. Pick a chair in the second row in the center and find an empty small drinking glass and a folded napkin at my place setting. Slowly open napkin. Find only a knife and a fork. Bad sign. Bye bye, coconut pie.

Two women next to me complain they can't see the screen from their seats. They leave. Check my deodorant. Not sure. Make note to shower next week.

Room quickly fills up with people mostly in their forties to sixties but a sprinkling of grey heads. I'm the best-dressed person there. (It's not often I can say that.) No one else was intimidated by the warning about the dress code. Too late to go home and change. What the hell—carpe diem.

Moderator tells crowd to watch introductory slide show till noon commencement of seminar. Slides show history of Internet and quotes inspirational words, "Some people dream of success while others wake up and work hard at it." Feel inspired. Raring to go. I could eat a horse.

11:50 p.m. Guy in front of me gets up and goes out. Returns with two muffins from the hotel's vending machine. Realize that no food served till 1:30 p.m. Regret not having a bigger breakfast. Wonder what they'll serve. I cross my fingers and look toward heaven. His muffins look scrumptious. The guy upstairs helps those who help themselves.

12:00 p.m. Moderator starts. He's great—combining the best of a gospel preacher, motivator, patent medicine pitchman, and comedian. Keeps the audience involved by asking questions, and this forces guests to respond out loud or raise their hand. Woman behind me has a raspy-shrill voice and shouts out a reply to every one of his questions for the next ninety minutes. Like to choke her. Decide not to, as she seems to be a favorite of the moderator.

Decide to join in and shout out answers to moderator's questions, such as "Do you want to have more money?" I got that one right. Feel exalted. Stifle urge to yell out, "Hallelujah." He's a spellbinder. (Maybe he can cure my athlete's foot. Maybe that's what an MP3 player does.)

There's electricity in the air. No smell of food. I'd trade electricity for a lamb chop.

Subject of presentation is "How to Make Money By Selling on the Internet." Sponsor is a public company that sells software that is supposed to help customers set up a Web site and then market their product(s). No questions allowed until the end. Man asks, "Why?" He's stared down, but good.

First subtle indication of trouble to come was the moderator's announcement that the drawing for the Dell laptop computer would include not only attendees at this seminar, but at all their seminars in South Florida. Dreams of a new laptop went up in smoke in a smoke-free environment. Man next to me murmurs, "Kiss that laptop good-bye, honey." "Honey" nods in agreement.

12:30 p.m. First mention of cost. $199 for CD to set up a Web site. Plus $24.95 per month for support and maintenance. Not bad. "Gets better," he smiles.

Sponsor magnanimously waives the $199 for anyone who signs up today to come to a full day's instructional seminar ten days hence at the same hotel and pays $58 now for that day (lunch included). Seems like a good deal. Save $199. Wonder what they'll serve for lunch. Roast beef for sure.

12:45 p.m. He then lowers the boom. Moderator says the Web site that you get for free (see 12:30 p.m.) is pretty good, but likens it to a man who wants to build a picket fence with stakes, nails, and a hammer. He can get the job done in a week or so of hard labor, but if he spent a few hundred dollars more, he could buy a battery-operated power nail driver and complete the job in a fraction of the time.

"Which would you want to do, use a hammer and take weeks to build your fence, or buy an expensive nail driver and finish in an hour?" he asks. Most of the audience leaps to its feet, shouting, "Buy the expensive nail driver."

Thought I noticed a slight smile on his shaman-like visage, but it was gone in a second—as was any smile on the audience's faces when the moderator says that if you want a really good Web site, you have to buy his company's Pro version for an additional $3,800. The room grows silent as if the air has been sucked out it. Thought to myself, they better serve steak for lunch if they expect people to dish out $3,800. Hope moderator can't read my mind. Wouldn't bet on it, the way he looks at me.

1:00 p.m. Man starts eating muffins. A few crumbs drop to the floor. Resist temptation. Stomach growls. Woman next to me gets up and changes seat.

1:01 p.m. Moderator recaps and holds up form people have to sign today to get in on the $58 special. Cash, credit card, or check. That's why they said to bring an ID to the seminar.

1:25 p.m. Waiters enter room carrying a plate for each participant. Cold turkey (deli type) on croissant, potato salad, and a large cookie. Wish I had an anti-depressant.

Never found out why they had given us a knife. Hari-kari? To add insult to injury, I had eaten turkey at dinner last night and brought home leftovers for tonight's meal. That makes three turkey meals in a row. Pitcher of cold water provided our beverage—free refills.

1:30 p.m. Many people were signing up. Walk out clutching my mail-in coupon for the possibly therapeutic MP3 player. Fine print says *shipping and handling not included. Figures. Couple walks out ahead of me; he was wearing shorts. Figures.*

When I got back home, I opened the fridge, ate a piece of pie, took a nap and dreamed of becoming a CIA agent.

PS. I did some added research on my own time and learned the sponsor and its parent are listed on the American Stock Exchange and have revenues of about $70 million. Most of their business is generated from free lunch seminars. They must have given away tens of thousands of cold turkey sandwiches.

The company's online support offices seem to be located in India. Maybe sandwiches come from a deli there.

I found there was a site on the Web devoted mainly to complaints from people who have attended this company's seminars. Also learned there is a class action suit and a suit or threats by several states' Attorneys General, plus Better Business Bureau complaints galore in the US and even in Australia.

California Attorney General and Ventura County District Attorney have settled a case brought against the company and accused it of violating consumer protection laws that have taken advantage of at least one hundred people in Ventura County.

The settlement required the company to pay $1.7 million. The company was banned from doing business in California in 2007. Not sure if it still banned. Their turkey sandwiches should be.

I went online to the complaint Web site and wrote that I didn't care about the lawsuits. I complained that people were paying too little attention to the quality of the turkey sandwiches. Received quite a few rude comments for my efforts. Glad I didn't use my right name.

I then called the company's headquarters to ask a question. Put on hold; then recorded voice (not with Indian accent) told me to call the firm's public relations firm. I called; the receptionist told me that the PR firm no longer serviced that account. I called back the company; the message still insisted I call the PR firm. Left my phone number with machine at company. They never called me.

My lawyer insisted that I add this disclaimer: Anything I have written or that might be implied from my description of the company in no way means to infer: that the services or products they are offering are not worth every penny they charge, or that the MP3 player that so many people complained they didn't get or didn't like wasn't worth every penny of the S&H charge, or that the turkey wasn't every bit as good as Boar's Head, or that the moderator was anything but a sweet guy, with a heart of $1,400 gold.

SENIORS ADVISED TO SPIT OUT FREE LUNCH

AARP and the North American Securities Administrators Association issued a report, "Protecting Older Investors: 2009 Free Lunch Seminar Report," which details that six million Americans age fifty-five or older attended a free lunch or dinner investment seminar over the past three years. I felt depressed when I read this report, because it meant I missed out on at least 5,999,992 free lunches.

Three-quarters of those who attended these seminars expected that the seminar would educate them about financial issues and strategies to help ensure a comfortable retirement. Instead, according to AARP, seminar attendees "…are pitched financial products that are fraudulent or unsuitable for them." The most commonly pitched products are variable annuities and equity-indexed annuities, both of which pay egregiously high commissions to the salesman and are wrongly described as low-risk/high-yield investments. Since three-quarters of the attendees in this study had these high expectations, I can only assume that one-quarter, or 1.5 million people, just went for the free food. Made me feel I was not alone.

What strikes me as particularly distressing about this extensive report is that there isn't one word about either the poor quality of the food or the undersized portions that some of these sponsors try to pass off as lunch or dinner. I believe there should be standards set up by AARP. Every organization that wants to offer a free lunch seminar should have to submit a menu thirty days in advance. This menu should be posted on AARP's Web site so a senior citizen can make an informed judgment as to whether to go or not.

To help reduce this type of abusive selling and increase awareness of fraudulent promotions, AARP has created the "Free Lunch Monitor" program and encourages individuals to call in and join the program. Each monitor receives a form to fill out whenever he or she attends such a seminar. Since I'm going to these seminars in the course of my research, I decided that I would try to assist AARP's project. I called and asked to be signed up as a monitor. I figured it would be prestigious to become an accredited free lunch monitor. The voice asked how I old I was. "Eighty-four," I replied. "You're too old," she said and hung up.

INTERMEZZO #1

I have decided to add a change of pace to this story of my adventures as a free lunch junkie by inserting, every now and then, comments on any range of subjects that may or not bear any direct relationship to the world of seminars. It's sorta like the thing fancy restaurants do when they serve a small dish of sorbet to cleanse the palate in between courses at a gourmet meal. Well, here goes.

Speaking of *scams* here in South Florida, let's talk Turkey.

I'll tell you about a personal experience I had when Judy and I were on a wondrous cruise of Turkey and the Greek Isles quite a few years ago. There weren't any free lunches on that trip, I can assure you.

We first visited the mother of all scams, the Trojan Horse. A giant recreation of the original stands several stories high on the site of that epic battle—a sight to remember. Every high-yielding variable annuity salesman reads this story to his children at bedtime.

Our next fabulous port of call was Kusadasi, Turkey, just for the day, starting at 8:00 a.m. A bus took us to the fantastic ruins at Ephesus. Our tour group spent the morning walking around the glorious ruins (an oxymoron to be sure), dating back to centuries before Christ. I decided to stay for the afternoon while the rest of the group went back to the ship, which was to sail at 5:00 p.m. Judy wasn't too pleased about my decision to go it alone in a foreign country, but I prevailed and took some wonderful panoramic pictures that afternoon. A little after 4:00 p.m. I decided it was time to wend my way back the twenty miles to the ship. I walked beyond the gates of the site and held up my thumb to try to hitch a ride ("hitch *bir* yolculuk" for those of you who speak Turkish.)

A dirty old Volkswagen-sized car sped past me, but the driver slammed on the brakes and backed the dusty car back to where I was standing. I asked if they would give me a lift to a bus stop so that I could get back to the ship. They spoke English. I got into the cramped back seat in which a dusty young boy was scrunched. The two men in the front were dressed in local workmen's garb (squalid sheets). One of them told me he had just left work at the excavation site and was heading home. Let's call him Gyorgy, which means, "earth worker."

He asked if I had any interest in rare old coins and just to be polite, I said yes. Gyorgy furtively pulled out a handful of dust-covered coins, which he said he had smuggled out of the "dig" that day. They looked pretty authentic to me, especially after he told me how many thousands of dollars they were worth. The earth worker said he would sell me the lot (excluding one special coin) for only $500. I began to feel a little uncomfortable. All of a sudden it hit me. They were gypsies, but I still believed there was a slight chance their story was true. I told him I wasn't a coin collector, but he didn't believe me. He said he was desperate to have the money today, so he would sell them for half price, $250. I got a sudden rush. Here was my chance to take advantage of a gypsy.

I always have had a knack for bargaining, so when I had bargained him down to $50, I felt I'd better buy them. But I made him include the special coin (to which his partner vociferously objected, which made me feel all the more certain that the coins were real). He finally acquiesced and agreed to drive me back to the boat as part of the deal. I told you I was a pretty good bargainer.

On the way he stopped at his mother's hovel. There he tried to coerce me into buying an "ancient gold" coin that she took out of a dirty cloth. I was tempted to seal the deal, but I didn't want to take advantage of an old lady.

The ride back to the ship was enlivened by the Turkish police, who had installed a blockade on the road looking for drivers who didn't have their cars properly registered, like, as it so happens, our driver. He spat out a curse, *"Tir Git"*, but I had no trouble understanding him. (Please don't go googling to translate this curse.) He had to pay a fine on the spot. It was just about the sum I had paid Gyorgy.

You can be sure the fine he paid to the policeman never made it past the local *taverna*.

While we were stopped at the checkpoint, I was told to hide the coins. I got a little more nervous. After passing through the blockade, the son graciously offered to sell me a coin from his private collection for only $2. His father seemed quite annoyed when I declined. I made it back to the ship on time and kept the coins in a vault for the rest of the voyage. I didn't have to declare the coins when we went through Customs because they were antiques.

Upon our return to Florida, I took the coins to a rare coin dealer, but I'm not sure he was much of an expert in coins this old— because he laughed at me. I made a necklace out of three of the coins for Judy for her birthday, but she only wears it on very special occasions. Otherwise we keep it in the safe in our house.

FREE BREAKFAST SEMINAR

Those three words were emblazoned in large type across the top of an ad in an advertising pullout section of my newspaper. I admit that a "free breakfast' is scraping the bottom of the barrel in my business, but you have to play the cards you're dealt.

However, as I read the smaller print in the ad, I began to lose my appetite, because it was "…for those seriously interested in pre-arranging a local in-ground or above-ground burial."

The sponsor was a local Jewish Memorial Chapel in affiliation with a Delray Beach Temple.

I visualized a buffet breakfast spread out alongside a neat row of gleaming coffins—each one trying to outshine its neighbor—like a stray at an animal shelter. Would it be a "hot breakfast" or just "casket continental cuisine"? I figured the chances of the chef at the Memorial Chapel serving up a buffet of all-you-can-eat bagels, cream cheese, Nova Scotia salmon, and whitefish were pretty slim.

Why should I ruin a perfectly good morning? Especially since the seminar was called for 10:00 a.m., which meant I wouldn't see a scrap of food until 11:00 a.m., for sure. If one of my freeloading friends saw me at a free breakfast seminar, I'd be pretty embarrassed. You have to have standards.

I wondered if I could call and ask what they were serving. I dropped the ad in the wastebasket.

STEAK AT LAST

When the call came through confirming my reservation for a free dinner seminar at Ruth's Chris, I felt as if I had been called up from the minor leagues to the big time. Visions of a porterhouse "grilled to perfection at 1,800 degrees and topped with fresh butter so that it sizzles all the way to your table" danced in my mind. I couldn't help salivating.

In addition, my excitement was heightened by the fact that the seminar was being sponsored by a firm that in June 2009 had been charged by the SEC with fraudulent sales practices for their alleged roles in fraudulent and unsuitable sales of variable annuities to senior citizens who were lured through free lunch seminars at restaurants in South Florida. Sounds like my kind of guys. They wound up paying about $600,000.

The seminar is being held almost exactly one year after the SEC's charges. I wonder if at the seminar the waiters will wheel in a huge cake with six thousand candles to mark the occasion.

My spirits were dampened a bit when I called the restaurant to ask about parking. "It's $8," a pleasant voice responded, explaining, "It's not our fault, the parking is handled by the county's concessionaire." I inquired if there was other parking available and was told that there was a parking lot around the corner that only charged $2 for the first two hours.

Another negative is that this seminar was to be held in West Palm Beach, and I live in Boca Raton. Did you know that you can go to MapQuest and not only get directions but also find out the estimated fuel cost? Well, it turns out that my fuel cost for the round trip would be about $12. Add this to their parking charge, and my visions of a "free" dinner evaporated faster than a drop of water in an 1,800-degree oven.

And since the seminar was called for 3:30 p.m., that meant dinner would be served at about *4:30* p.m. Another early, early bird dinner. The restaurant opens to the public at 5:00 p.m. for dinner. I was pretty sure that I'd be able to get back to the parking lot within the two-hour minimum and avoid having to pay for the third hour, but I'd have to stay on my toes (and that's where my athlete's feet is the worst).

I made up my mind to make my Ruth's Chris experience a day to remember. So at 12:15 p.m. I headed to Steak n' Shake for lunch with my discount coupon in hand for their double cheeseburger and fries. Delicious. I didn't spring for a strawberry shake because I didn't want to fill up before my dinner, which was less than three hours away. I also learned how to become a member of their exclusive "Steak n' Shake Club" and earn future awards. I hope they accept me.

I still had a few hours to kill, so I decided to spiff myself up for the seminar. I didn't want to look like some loser who was just looking for a free meal, so I headed to my barber. I have been patronizing the same shop for the past twenty years that I have lived in Florida. You might think that I was attracted solely by the price (then $6 now $10), but that's not the only reason. This shop isn't some fancy emporium where they have ditsy blondes giving "sissy" manicures or where they wash your hair—I can wash my own hair very well, thank you. I realize that all my friends *tip* their barber more than I pay for my haircut, but I like the laid-back, no-frills atmosphere. I'm in and out in less than ten minutes. It costs about a buck a minute.

Back in my car with still time to kill. I spied a Big Lots store across the street. What could be more fitting than a shopping spree in an off-price closeout retailer? I grabbed a shopping cart and gazed at the "extraordinary bargains" and "amazingly low prices." My eyes came to rest on some cans of cat food, which were marked down to $1 a tin. As I read the label, I wondered if our cat (Kittles) would mind that the "best if used by" date was months ago. And could I get them by Judy's inspection? I chose to pass up the bargain and sadly left the store empty-handed.

I was back in the car with time to spare so I headed north on the turnpike at 40 mph. Cars whooshed by me, but I didn't care, because I didn't want to pull into the parking lot too early and incur a charge for an additional hour. I mused over how, as I was about to leave the house, Judy had once again criticized my attire. I explained to her that it was difficult to dress properly when I was having lunch at Steak n' Shake and dinner at Ruth's Chris. And I was sure that with my spiffy haircut, no one would be looking at my clothes.

I arrived at the restaurant at 2:45 p.m. and drove quickly past the "Valet Parking $8" sign and followed the arrows to the municipal parking lot, which turned out to be at least five very long blocks past the restaurant. I didn't want to enter the garage before 3:10 p.m., so I pulled into an alley and parked. It gave me time to rehearse what excuse I was going to give the moderator of the seminar for not setting up an appointment to meet with him to buy whatever annuity he was selling.

The garage was empty. I found a spot near the exit, and my parking ticket read 3:11 p.m. Not bad timing. When I started my trek back to the restaurant, the Florida summer sun and its ninety-three-degree temperature and humidity engulfed me. There wasn't any shade on the sidewalk as far as the eye could see. I wished I had brought suntan lotion. I felt like a Jewish Lawrence of Arabia. It took over ten minutes to negotiate the five blocks of sunbaked sidewalk to the welcoming lobby of the air-conditioned restaurant.

The restaurant's pretty, sleek hostess (who had been poured into a skintight black frock) looked like a mirage. Since the seminar was not ready to start, she asked me to be seated. I told her I'd do anything she asked. I wondered if she noticed my haircut. I thought of going to the men's room, but wondered if there would be a smiling attendant there with a towel in one hand and an outstretched palm in the other. I was lucky, no palms in sight. Muzak in the toilet. I only wish they had magazines.

I sat with other dinner guests in the garish waiting area, with faux Chihulys on the wall. I wondered what he (Dale Chihuly) would think if he came in. A woman asked for a menu while we waited. I wanted to do the same to check out the prices, but I didn't want to look as if I had never been here before.

3:25 p.m. Check in. Enter small private room. Four tables cramped in. I bet the Angus cows that rode to Chicago (to become our sirloins) had more room in their cattle car than we do.

An array of highly polished silverware sits at parade rest on a field of starched white tablecloths. You don't have to consult the Oracle at Delphi to know we're in for a fine dining experience. Get a whiff of a steak charcoaling on the grill. It has my name on it, for sure.

Sit at a table with an older couple; actually, everyone is an older couple.

Menu on table. Salad, choice of six-ounce filet, chicken or crab cakes. Mashed potatoes and creamed spinach as sides. Plus cake and berries and cream. No beverage, but glass of water with four slices of lime on the table. Can't have everything.

"Medium, and hold the butter," I say nonchalantly to the waitress, trying to appear like a regular. (Ruth douses her steaks with butter to harden whatever arteries the meat doesn't. Now I know why an unmarked ambulance was parked outside.)

I mentally estimate the cost of my dinner—not a penny less than $45. I smile. I'll still be able to show a profit after deducting the parking and gas.

3:40 p.m. Couple at my table smile shyly and put on their name-tags. Me too. Somehow conversation turns to exorbitant valet parking charge and glad to find he also passed it up for the cheaper municipal garage. Tells me about a shortcut that's not in the sun for my return to the parking garage. Says only gone to three or four seminars in past five years. Says going to Europe this summer.

Speaker enters. A young lawyer. Discloses that his partner in branch office is an accountant. He's not the guy mentioned in the SEC complaint. Firm has thirty-five offices. Wonder if each office has a free lunch seminar I could attend.

Apologizes for the small, cramped room. Says usually have a much nicer room. Everyone willing to forgive him. Apologizes for starting ten minutes late, but guarantees dinner will still start on time at 4:30 p.m.— someone sighs. Speaker tells about his firm and their financial and tax planning services. Uses PowerPoint to illustrate his lecture. Bet he could show me how to use my VCR.

Offers free one-hour visit to review your tax returns, will, stock and bond portfolio, and I'm not sure, but I think I heard he included a review of your last chest X-ray. Maybe not, but it's hard to concentrate when I'm consumed with wondering if my six-ounce filet will be cooked just right.

No mention of annuities. Guess SEC finished that off.

4:20 p.m. Comes to end ten minutes early, but no one seems to mind. Recaps his company's advantages. Beseeches audience that if they sign up and come to his office for his free one-hour session, they don't take in all his advice and then go back to their original adviser or attorney. Says he paid a lot for the dinner.

Someone's stomach growls.

His assistant comes to each person to set up an appointment. My tablemate says he will set up date on his return to Florida. Some pressure to make date now. He resists. Tells me he does need a lawyer and will be calling. I believe him. I'm impressed; they're not freeloaders. Quality people.

I tell his assistant that I'm going north and can't make an appointment till November. Assistant says that's OK because speaker is going to be in the New York area in July. I say going to Nome, Alaska. If looks could kill.

Everyone else passes on making a firm appointment. Assistant losing patience. Not sure, but believe my tablemate is the only one going to follow up.

4:35 p.m. Salad appears, followed by main course and dessert. Steak cooked just right. Plate sizzles. I'd recommend this seminar to anyone. They do refill water glasses. Could use a fresh lemon wedge but decide to re-squeeze the sprig I was allotted.

Flabbergasted when my tablemates get up to leave before dessert is served. They have another appointment. Wonder if I should ask waitress to doggie bag their desserts for me. I'd be toast if Judy found out I'd eaten my cake and theirs too. Speaker doesn't stay around after his talk to mingle and drum up business. Guess he wants to get his car out of the garage within the two-hour special price period.

5:15 p.m. I finish dinner, grab menu, and rush out.

I didn't make it back to the garage in two hours and got a bill for $5.25. What the hell. I picked a bit of steak (medium rare) from my tooth. It was still flavorful. I headed for home. A few days later I received an e-mail informing me that I had been accepted into Steak 'n Shakes eClub, their "exclusive" (their word) online venue for special offers and coupons. I guess being a member of Sweet Tomatoes' online club greased the wheels of my membership application. I'm gradually building up an impressive list of memberships for my obituary.

One depressing thing about the online application form I had to fill in for Steak 'n Shakes' Club was that the pull-down window to enter my *year* of birth only went back to 1930. This is blatant age discrimination, but instead of being a whistle-blower, I checked off "1930" and let it go at that. Judy surmised that they cut off people born before 1930 because anyone beget prior to 1930 who had been eating at Steak n' Shake all those years would be dead by now.

AGE DISCRIMINATION

The offer in the mail seemed too good to be true:
TWO COMPLIMENTARY ROUND-TRIP AIRFARES
3 day/ 2-night Hotel at Hilton or Marriot
$100 Dining Certificate

I grabbed the phone and called the 866 number. I was put on hold. With an offer this good I wasn't surprised that there was a wait. Finally, after what seemed like an eternity, a kindly voice on the other end said that all my wife and I had to do to qualify for the free offers was to listen to a ninety-minute presentation given by a travel agency. This sure seemed a small-enough price to pay for such a wonderful vacation. I wondered if there was a Hilton in Hawaii. But some things she said didn't seem to ring true.

"Wait," the voice said, sounding a bit less friendly. "There are three qualifications." *I knew the offer seemed too good to be true.*

1. Both Judy and I had to be between the ages of thirty-nine and eighty-one. I failed the first prerequisite, and I failed it on the wrong side.

I naturally thought about lying about my age, but the voice anticipated my venality and informed me that two forms of ID were required. I wondered how much a fake driver's license would cost and how long it would take to make one. But since one of my sons and his wife work for Homeland Security, I decided against that ploy.

For the life of me I couldn't figure out why any self-respecting scammer wouldn't be willing to fleece everyone, regardless of age. Very suspicious indeed. Un-American. If I had a whistle, I'd blow it in her ear. Then the voice told me the two other qualifications:

2. Judy and I had to have a combined income of $40,000. Why did the rip-off artist not want to pick the pockets of people earning less than 40K? Must be a liberal, communist, or even worse, an Obamacrat.

3. We both must be US citizens and be able to read and write English.

Soon you'll have to show your ID and take an oath of allegiance before you can buy an overpriced timeshare.

JUDY MEETS HELEN OF TROY
IN NEIMAN MARCUS

We received a $50 free gift card (in the mail) from Neiman Marcus (in the mall) good for lunch in their Mariposa Restaurant. Now I know how the citizens of Troy felt when they received the giant horse as a present from the Greeks a few millenniums ago.

While I really enjoy the kitchen's giant steaming hot popovers, the risk of having to shepherd Judy in and then out of Neiman without her finding some adorable thing that will cost me more than the free lunch is almost insurmountable.

To make matters worse we had to take separate cars because Judy had a bridge date after lunch. This meant she'd be on her own, walking through the counters brimming with alluring, perhaps irresistible "necessities of life in Boca." Off we went. I met up with my wife at the dining room. She wasn't carrying any packages—but she could have had them delivered or stored. (I thought of doing a strip search.) Lunch was delicious and with tip, the check came to exactly $50. Off we went on our separate ways. That evening Judy came home all excited. She had had a few minutes free before bridge and went into another store, which was having a giant sale. She was able to find a beautiful pair of slacks, originally listed at $115, which were on sale for $19, and the saleslady said she could take off an additional 20 percent. Naturally she scooped them up. I told her I didn't think it was right for her to take advantage of the poor storeowner that way, and that she should return them. She wore them to dinner that night. I wondered if Helen ever bought togas on sale.

TAKE THIS WITH A GRAIN OF SALT
(Kosher, s'il vous plaît)

Some of my readers might take umbrage at my taking advantage of the sponsors (scammers excluded) of the free lunch seminars who paid for my meal when I had no intention of buying their product. However, my conscience is clear because I'm sure that the sponsors of these seminars realize that there will always be some lowlife who attends just to get a free meal, so it might as well be me.

I also add in my defense that I go to these seminars with an open mind. I have already laid out tens of thousands of dollars to buy a long-term health-care policy for Judy that I learned about at one of these free lunch seminars. And if something else good comes along* while I'm chewing on my filet, I certainly will consider it. Not a pig in a poke, not some half-baked scheme, not something you have to take with a grain of salt, but a plan that will make my mouth water. I'm as eager as the next man to get in on the gravy train, and I'm looking for something that will sell like hotcakes.

If these idioms don't convince you of my sincerity, I'll make a deal with you. I'll show you I'm not a bad egg. If I make a killing selling this book (any profit of over $100 would qualify) I promise to reimburse every one of my benefactors in kind. I guarantee to provide a free lunch (without any speeches) to each and every scam-less sponsor whose seminar I attended. In addition, I will offer to sell copies of my book at a 20 percent discount. No age restrictions. One-year time limit.

- In September I visited a doctor whose seminar I had attended. He charged a bundle.

WHERE'S THE BEEF?

Did you know that July 9 is *Cow Appreciation Day*? Some advertising genius at Chick-fil-A dreamed up the franchise's national advertising campaign, which features talking cows that are grateful for people who eat at Chick-fil-A because the chain's 1,600 stores *don't serve hamburgers*.

And to commemorate the campaign, for the past six years the fast-food franchise has given a free meal to anyone who shows up at their counter on July 9 dressed as a cow. Supposedly more than 300,000 customers donned cow costumes last year, but that might be a lot of bull. I happened upon this item in the paper on July 8.

I mused that if I go to a seminar and endured a one-hour-plus presentation on some boring subject to snag a free meal, I surely can dress up as a cow and present myself at Chick-fil-A's in Boca Raton. But I didn't have a cow costume in my closet, and the fateful day was less than twenty-four hours away. Talk about quandaries.

As I read further in the newspaper article, my spirits picked up, because there was a Plan B. If I showed up at the counter wearing a cow-spotted scarf, or other cow accessory, I would still qualify for a free entrée—not quite as big a deal as the complete meal (an entrée, one side, and a soft drink) I'd earn dressed as a cow, but still it's not chopped liver. For my non—Jewish readers who never heard the expression "It's not chopped liver," you can substitute "It's not pork rinds."

I found a cowbell in the garage, and Judy made a necklace so that I could hang it around my neck. I set off on my pilgrimage, proud to be a participant in my first Cow Appreciation Day. Julia Childs couldn't have felt any more excited when she set off for La Tour D'Argent.

I expected to find a line around the block in front of the Chick-fil-A counter, with hordes of cow-dressed Floridians licking their chops in breathless anticipation of a free fowl feast. Imagine my surprise when I found *no lines* at their store in the mall, *no cows*, just a few young chicks.

I embarrassedly strode up to the young lady behind the lunch counter, showed her my necklace, and went, "Moo." "You're my first Cow Appreciation Day customer," she mooed back. I surveyed the extensive menu board emblazoned on the back wall. There were so many choices that I asked her which was the best. "Chicken #1," she replied, brushing back a straggly cowlick. I nodded OK to her suggestion, and ten seconds later gathered in my prize.

I wanted to have my picture taken with the Chick-fil-A costumed cow, but was told the "cow" was on a bathroom break. (I had visions of the "cow" walking around in the parking lot looking for a grassy area.)

Then I pulled up a chair to enjoy my lunch in the food court. As I looked around, I noticed two things. First, there were a few young girls dressed as cows wolfing down their entrée, side, and drink; and second, on the menu board the Chicken #1 was the cheapest item on the list ($3.04). The counter girl had deviously steered me away from the Chicken #7 Deluxe ($4.69). There's always next year.

Finally the "cow" showed up. It had a piece of toilet paper on the bottom of one of its shoes. I guessed it had found a comfort station.

The author is on the left.

In retrospect, I saved a cow and killed a chicken. I wonder where Al Gore stands on this issue.

YOU CAN'T WIN THEM ALL

The next day got off to a bad start, a harbinger of things to come. A toothache spoiled my night's sleep. Then I spent almost an hour on the phone chatting with one of Spirit Airlines' reservation clerks located in the Philippines as I tried to book a Frequent Flyer Award flight. Between his accent and my slight hearing deficiency, the international dialogue sounded a little like an Abbott and Costello "Who's on first?" routine. I don't know which was more debilitating, the toothache or trying to understand him. As the conversation dragged on, I got even more agitated, since my 1:00 p.m. free lunch seminar was drawing near.

Finally at ten to one I finished talking with my adversary in the Far East and raced off to Bonefish Grill. This branch was located in Boca. The parking lot was crowded, but fortunately I found a spot before I had to use valet parking. Breathlessly I entered the restaurant. Would I be too late and be turned away empty-stomached?

"Not too late," smiled the jacket, shirt, and tie. "Have a seat anywhere." I viewed a large room with tables set up in the shape of a *U*. I took the nearest seat and filled in the proffered form with address, phone number, and other vitals. Other people straggled in for the next ten minutes or so. I was sorry I rushed. The table was set for twenty-four people, but four or five no-showed. Why in the world would anyone not show up for a free lunch at Bonefish Grill? You can't play shuffleboard in this heat.

1:05 p.m. Fill out the form and lie about my age, because can't remember if there was an age restriction on the invite. Look around and realize I'm not the oldest. Mostly couples dressed as if they just stepped out of a fashion window at Walmart. My Sy Syms outfit a stunner. Judy would die.

Open my napkin. Includes knife and two forks. Good sign—either salad or dessert—I'm rooting for dessert. Waitress offers soft drink or iced tea. No menu. Bad sign. I don't like fish and especially salmon, but at Bonefish Grill I can't expect steak.

It's cold. Put on sweater. No one else has a sweater or jacket. They must not be used to going to a restaurant for lunch in the summer in Boca. Several ask to have air turned down. Never happens. Woman puts napkins over arms. No one will fall asleep here.

The battery on my wristwatch went on the blink that morning, so the times I list for the events in the narrative that follows are approximate. Having nothing to do with this seminar, but my mood is darkened because my fax is out, the pool skimmer doesn't work, the circuit breaker for half the electricity in the house is out, and my tooth hurts.

1:15 p.m. Speaker steps into the arena. Fortyish, pleasant, carnival barker. Welcomes all and goes around the U asking each person's first name and writing it on the paper tablecloth as a reminder for him. Banters with each guest. Develops rapport. Smiles all around. He's a spellbinder. Has people eating out of the palm of his hand. Wish he had a hamburger there.

Mentions George Steinbrenner died this morning at age eighty. A few people shudder, and Red Sox fan smiles.

1:22 p.m. Gives his background. Says he's being graded today. Points to man in back of room who is now standing, but who I notice was served lunch awhile ago. Big Wheel!

Pulls up erasable chalkboard. Says purpose of his talk is to "... earn forty-five minutes of your time some day in the future." Asks how many people have attended seminars in the past. A few forks are raised, but not mine, due to temporary paralysis (will go away on first sight of lunch.)

1:30 p.m. Declares stocks, bonds, real estate, Munis, REITS, CDs all bad investments! Only indexed annuities are safe and provide growth. Several in audience chime in that they have annuities. He asks, "How old are the policies?" They tell him.

"Newer ones are better," he retorts "and my annuities eliminate the downside, accentuate the positive."

"What are the negatives?" dour man asks. "None!" He responds triumphantly.

Speaker says he's getting 8 percent guaranteed and no risk. That gets everyone's attention.

"What are the costs?" lady with napkin around her shoulders asks.

".43 percent per annum," he responds.

Crowd murmurs its approval. My stomach growls. Iced tea refilled without asking. I haven't had a bite to eat in seven hours. Wonder how long a person can go without food. May find out today.

He keeps asking questions of audience. "Earl, what did Einstein say was the greatest invention of all time?" I wonder if he thinks I know the answer because Albert and I are both Jewish.

"Don't know," I confess. "Compound interest," he replies.

"Could have fooled me," I respond. "I guess it's all relative." He dirty looks me.

People keep getting up to go to the bathroom. Maybe warmer in there. Maybe they need Flomax. Maybe there's a snack vending machine in bathroom.

Woman gets up and goes out the front door. A few minutes later she returns with a sweater. Soon the color returns to her face.

Wonder if I should go next door and buy a sandwich. Wonder if he would be offended if I ate a bologna sandwich while he talked about 8 percent annuities. Could kill two birds if I ate a chicken sandwich.

Scribbling away furiously, and no one else is taking a single note. Afraid he'll ask me what the hell I'm doing. Get answer ready. I'll tell him I have slight case of Alzheimer's and want to be able to remember what he said. If he does ask me this question, to prove that I'm a little addled, I'll ask him if lunch has already been served.

2:10 p.m. Speaker turns to his assistant in back and asks how much lead time do we have to give the kitchen to get ready to serve lunch. Response is, "Ten minutes."

"OK, tell them to start."

Pulse starts to race. Guests open up their napkins. I bring my fork to the ready position. He keeps talking, emphasizing the importance of meeting with him for forty-five minutes at some later date.

2:30 p. m. I keep watching the kitchen door. I intone, "Abracadabra, open sesame," and as if by magic the door opens, and waiter brings in bread with pesto sauce. Grab basket from in front of my neighbor and devour half a loaf. She looks at me...just as Judy does sometimes.

Lunch arrives. Small piece of chicken on mashed potatoes and small piece of salmon. Gulp down chicken and taters. Try salmon. Can't eat it. Hate salmon.

Ask for more bread. Dirty look.

Ask waitress if there is dessert. She gives me mother of all dirty looks.

As wipe a scrap of bread from my mouth, speaker comes to my setting, looks me in the eye, and asks, "Earl, what days are you free?"

"Wednesday afternoons are good for me," I reply.

"Great, I just happen to have this Wednesday afternoon free," he answers. Moment of truth. Feel like Wyatt Earp staring down an outlaw

in a duel in Gunfight in the O.K. Corral. I pull the trigger—"I can't make it tomorrow, and I don't have my calendar book with me, so I'm not sure what day I'm free, but please call me to set up an appointment."

He's heard that line hundreds of times before. Ask myself if I should mention that I don't eat salmon. Decide discretion, etc.

Lightning and thunder outside. Very appropriate.

He shrugs his shoulders and surrenders. Puts pen back in holster and leaves my info sheet, which has my phone number on it, on the table and goes down the row from person to person. Wonder if I could swipe my info sheet without his noticing and skip out the door. Biggest decision I've had to make in a long time. What would Gordon Gekko do? Chicken out and duck out empty-handed. Wonder if they'll get some turkey to stake out my house to see when I'm free to have an appointment with the speaker.

Exited restaurant hungry but smiling, because it is raining, and my car is finally getting the wash it so richly deserves.

CONSUMED BY ADDICTION

I woke up the next morning with sweaty palms, the shakes and diluted pupils. I realized I was a "junkie" and that I had become addicted to "free lunch seminars" and I was experiencing severe withdrawal symptoms. My body craved a *free* filet cooked to perfection at 1800 degrees. My ears craved the siren-like sounds of a fast-talking huckster spewing forth info about annuities that were "too good to be true." I ate my heart out worrying where my next free meal would come from. My soul cried out for the companionship of other freeloaders as tablemates in a mahogany-paneled private room at a famous steak house. I thirsted for a free glass of a red wine with excellent color, good body and robust health, even though I am a teetotaler.

I needed a fix (a free filet).

I took to hanging around the mailbox waiting to see if I'd be getting any new invitations.

I drove to the local "Meat Emporium" and stared at the prime steaks in the window, but I didn't go in to make a purchase because I've learned from my adventures that a *free* filet tastes a lot better than the other variety.

I moped outside of Ruth's Chris, standing close to the front door so I could get a whiff of the steaks on the grill whenever someone went through the doorway.

I even chewed Nicorette gum, but all it did was make me want to start smoking again.

My hypnotist wasn't up to the task, either.

My psychiatrist listened to my complaints for 50 minutes and then asked if I'd take him along on my next seminar.

Well, I tried.

SHIP AHOY: TORPEDOED

Judy came rushing into my office excitedly waving a letter in front of me. She shouted, "We're going on a five-day/four-night cruise for *free* plus a bonus of a $300 Target Discount Certificate if we respond within seventy-two hours." "Start packing," I said, "and don't forget your bathing suit."

We'd soon be able to spend four days sailing on the high seas, eating from the sumptuous buffets, dancing under the stars, and visiting exotic ports of call.

The letter included a facsimile travel voucher for Royal Caribbean or Carnival Cruise Lines. The sponsor of this free giveaway was listed as a travel agency.

I continued reading:

NO GIMMICKS! THIS IS NOT A TIMESHARE SOLICITATION
Seating is limited and fills up fast.
Confirmation NUMBER 8602

The words in the ad "NO GIMMICKS" gave me a warm and fuzzy feeling. I could almost feel the pleasant sting of the ocean's salt spray on my face as I sipped a frozen daiquiri in my deck chair on my private balcony.

My reverie was broken by the realization that a torpedo was headed for our dream cruise ship. I suddenly remembered the name of the travel agency from an earlier free offer for a five-day/four-night vacation at any Marriot of our choice. If you have been paying attention, you'll also remember that when I called to book that vacation, I was told, "No one over eighty-one years of age is allowed."

I took a chance and called the 800 number. A young woman answered the phone. I disguised my voice, but she spelled out the age requirements for all applicants. Judy began to unpack.

I felt so badly about being excluded from the free five-night cruise that I decided to go to Carnival Cruise Line's Web site and see just what we were missing out on. The cheapest cabin was advertised for $169 per person, plus $67 for port fees and taxes for a five-day cruise to Mexico.

The small print on the reverse side of the facsimile travel voucher we had received included these words, "Couple is responsible for $149 per person port and other taxes." Some smaller print on Carnival's Web site revealed there was also a mandatory charge for tipping of $40 and a fuel surcharge of $36. Add it all up, and the free trip would cost $225 per person. No gimmicks!

Carnival said that they do not have available a photo of the $169 inside room. It seems the ship's photographer was claustrophobic and refused to enter the room. The ship's captain advised passengers who had a queasy feeling about being slid into a CAT scan machine to avoid booking an inside cabin.

But wait; to be fair, the free offer also included a $300 Target Customer Loyalty Rebate Certificate. The Palm Beach Post reported that under this program, if a customer spends $300 at Target, he'd get a $75 rebate card less a $12.50 handling charge. So the "$300 Target Discount Certificate" trumpeted in the ad is not what it's cracked up to be. Surprise! No gimmicks.

The newspaper article also mentioned that the Florida Attorney General's Office had received more than 240 complaints against the company that runs the free cruise deals for this travel agency. Two hundred and forty complaints is chickenfeed. (In the two months after the article appeared, the number of complaints had grown to 408.)

It's only fair to add that the agency's local president was quoted in the newspaper article describing the complaints of people who had attended their seminars as saying that the company had recently switched to another firm to handle their free cruise deals. I looked this new firm up with the Better Business Bureau. I can see why they switched. The new firm only had 111 complaints filed against them. In this business that makes them altar boys. But they were clear with Florida's Attorney General. I'll check back.

PS. Surprise. An affiliate of this travel agency sells timeshares in other seminars. I guess gimmicks are allowed.

DESPERATE TIMES REQUIRE
DESPERATE MEASURES

Things are so slow in the free lunch seminar business during the summer in South Florida that I almost jumped for joy when I spied an ad in the newspaper:

FREE LIVING WILL SEMINAR
COMPLIMENTRAY LUNCH WILL BE SERVED

As I read on I wondered why a seminar on living wills was being sponsored by a memorial park. The address was in Ft. Lauderdale, perhaps a thirty-minute drive, but DTRDM (see page heading).

The other problem was that this seminar was scheduled for 11:30 a.m., and I wasn't sure that I could get back to Boca in time for my 3:00 p.m. seminar that same day at Ruth's Chris—but the opportunity to have back-to-back free meals was too great to miss. Just like going to a Yankee vs. Red Sox doubleheader.

The telephone receptionist asked if I had a living will, a wife, and a cemetery plot. I answered no, yes, and no. Here I was only one minute into the conversation, and I had lied twice. She then said that the seminar would include a tour of their cemetery. Wow! What a way to spend a steamy summer afternoon.

I asked if the luncheon was served in the memorial park. "Yes," she answered. I visualized being served barbecued ribs that had been smoked in the crematorium with an organist playing Chopin's "Funeral March" in the background.

The voice at the other end of the phone asked if my wife was going to attend. I wanted to tell her that my wife wouldn't be caught dead at a free lunch seminar, but I thought that particularly inappropriate, and just said no. She asked who made the decisions in my family. I told her that I did if I was alone and my wife didn't find out. She laughed politely, but still pressured me to bring my wife. I struggled for a way out and fibbed that my wife had trouble walking. The receptionist's voice brightened as she responded, "We have excellent facilities for wheelchairs." I decided to get firm with her and answered, "If I have to bring my wife, you can cancel my reservation." She backed off, and I felt I had won a victory. But I knew how King Pyrrhus felt after defeating the Romans at Heraclea in 280 BC, since I'd still have to take a guided tour of the cemetery.

I wondered if they used a specially outfitted hearse as the tour vehicle. I wondered what I should wear. I wondered if I would choke on the barbecued ribs. I wondered whose ribs they would be. I wondered if I could request a vegetarian lunch.

I wondered if the cemetery was nonsectarian, so I went to the Web and found that Lauderdale Memorial Park was one of three cemeteries belonging to the City of Ft. Lauderdale. Their Internet site offered a video tour of the cemetery, but I decided not to spoil the excitement of seeing the burial plots up close and personal on my guided tour. I wondered if I could turn my free lunch seminar adventures into a reality TV series, perhaps starring that guy on the Food Channel who eats his way across the world.

IT'S A BEAUTIFUL PLACE TO VISIT, BUT...

It isn't often in life that a long-anticipated event exceeds your expectations. Well, I can honestly say that my free lunch seminar at a Ft. Lauderdale cemetery fit the bill. Amazingly enough, this happened despite the rainstorm I drove through on my thirty-five-minute drive to the memorial park. I was sure this was a foreboding of a difficult day ahead with my having to slog through the mud on a tour of the grounds. But "neither rain, nor snow…" kept this chronicler from the completion of his self-appointed task of finding the best food served at a cemetery in South Florida."

I knew I was taking a financial risk as I set off in my car at 10:30 a.m., because the round trip would consume almost four gallons of gas. (Which meant that the lunch would have to be worth at least $12 for me to break even.) But as I had nothing better to do, I decided I'd take the gamble.

My phone rang at 9:00 a.m. that morning—the cemetery seminar registrar checking on whether I'd be showing up or not. Her words worried me. She said she wanted to verify the number of guests before she ordered a "light" lunch. An optimist would react to this description by saying that since they're serving a "light" lunch, they won't be using the back burner of their crematorium to do the cooking. A pessimist would worry that a "light" lunch meant tuna on white (heavy on the mayo).

Traffic was light, and I arrived in the area fifteen minutes early, so I filled up my car's tank. (Gas is cheaper there.) Then I drove *the last mile* to the memorial park.

The sun broke through the clouds as I entered the cemetery. What a stunning vista. Beautiful entrance, massive, majestic banyan trees reached up toward heaven. Vast fields of green grass were sprinkled with bouquets of flowers set in small metal receptacles and a few marble benches. American flags waved proudly in the strong breeze. The sun's reflections bounced off the gravestones in a myriad of colors, and off in the distance a few monolithic mausoleums and a plain office structure.

What an idyllic setting for a picnic lunch.

No headstones could be found in this cemetery and the land is very flat, so there is quite a green panorama. Al Gore would love it there. Maybe Tipper would like to see him there. A row of pre-fabricated homes sat uneasily on their slabs across the street from the cemetery. Men worked on their early-model cars in the driveways. No garages. I wonder what it's like to live across the street from a cemetery (must be great on Halloween). Also, no need to pay for a hearse when Grandpa kicks the bucket. Just rest the casket on a few skateboards and push him across the street.

I wonder how they advertise one of these homes for sale:

"Great view. Especially nice when wind is blowing from the north. Live close to your parents. BYOSAS. (Bring your own shovel and save.)"

I parked my car, entered the one-story administrative building and was shown to an empty, small conference room that also served as a showroom for samples of the bronze mausoleum niche plates. I gazed up at the various stone and metal "nametags for the dead" lining the walls. Certainly not the décor I'd ordinarily choose for a place to have a quiet pastoral midday meal. Maybe, instead, they're going to serve a picnic lunch outdoors amidst the gravestones—or cook up a barbecue next to the crematorium. Hope springs eternal when you're in a cemetery.

Keithly Warner, a seventy-three-year-old retired priest, was led into the room and extended his hand. He was the first black guest I had encountered in my free lunch seminar excursions. I learned he is single, no children, and conservative in his religious leanings—solid as the rock of ages. He was born in Antigua and in his retirement has developed a love of cruises—three so far this year. He was attracted to this seminar because the bait for getting people to come to the seminar, besides the free meal, was an explanation of living wills.

Martha and John were brought in—a pleasant-looking older couple with the solid look of Midwestern churchgoers. They told us they once lived in Panama. He was an engineer. They wore their religion on their sleeves.

11:35 a.m. Isaac enters. Our speaker.
A middle-aged Israeli with an accent.
Kathy is his middle-aged assistant, sans accent.
Offers coffee. Won't be able to have my morning nap, so ask for black to ensure I don't fall asleep during the presentation.

Isaac asks our names and addresses. John can't remember his zip code. Smiles embarrassedly. Keithly and I shine—we remember ours.

Isaac says four parts to our seminar today: (1) pre-planning for death, (2) tour of grounds, (3) lunch, and (4) one-on-one meeting. Number four could be a bitch. Sure they'll match me up with Eli, and I'm no match for an Israeli.

Isaac asks if any of us has a living will. Everyone says, no. (I lied.) Isaac reads from booklet, "Ten Tools for Health Care Planning." He gets call on his cell. Apologizes and has to leave the room. Kathy takes over, but details of living wills are a bit out of her element, so she changes subject. Tells us city owns four cemeteries in Ft. Lauderdale. Each has its own distinctive style and atmosphere.

She works for New York Stock Exchange Company that manages the cemetery for the city. (When I got home, I checked them out on the Internet. They operate 145 funeral homes in twenty-five states and thirty-three cemeteries in twelve states.) *I smile. Surely such a big company can afford to provide quite a sumptuous lunch. Daydream of two-pound lobster swimming in butter and lemon. Hope they provide a bib; wearing a clean shirt.*

Kathy says the cemetery we are visiting is on city-owned land, which is important, because commercial cemeteries are on private land and one hundred years after they sell out the last plot, the whole kit and caboodle can be plowed under for condominiums. We all nod approvingly. Who wants to spend eternity under the basement of a condo? Ask Jimmy Hoffa.

She goes around the room asking each of us if we plan cremation or burial. John tells story of his father who died at an early age. Wipes tears away.

11:45 a.m. Isaac comes back and rescues Kathy. She tells him where he left off in the manual. Get the feeling we are behind schedule and so is lunch. More explanation of pre-planning for death.

Kathy chimes in with a comment and refers to me as Mr. Bernstein. Isaac corrects her.

12:30 p.m. Talk is over. Head for tour of grounds. The other three guests ride in a stretch golf cart with Isaac, while Kathy chauffeurs me in regular golf cart. She asks why I'm taking so many notes. Tell her my memory isn't what it used to be and want to be able to describe today's events to Judy. She believes me. Her eyes sparkle because I'm beginning to give the impression of being a likely prospect, and my advanced age makes her feel I'd better do something sooner rather than later.

The two carts drive side by side through the grounds, with Isaac pointing out the highlights. Reminds me of our safari in Tanzania. Isaac shows us special area for veterans—they get a discount—my ears perk up. Says big attendance on Memorial Day. Air Force used to have F-16 jets fly in close formation over the cemetery but cut back to two helicopters because of the lousy economy. Unless business improves, they'll probably use paper airplanes next year.

Isaac says each of the burial sections face in a different direction. Says that's good. Ask why. He says Muslims want to be buried facing Mecca. I ask, "Are there many Muslims buried here?" "Just a few." he replies. Can see he's sorry he raised the issue in the first place.

Off to mausoleum. Explains they are deep. Couple can be slid in to lay head to head. Sounds romantic. Can just hear Frank Sinatra crooning, "I'm in heaven when we're lying head to head."

Man drives up to nearby crypt. Puts fresh flowers in vase, along with powder to keep them fresh longer. Bows his head. Takes out handkerchief.

Isaac boasts that they are only cemetery in Florida to have bronze plaques available to mark your mausoleum bin. "Who would want to be buried anywhere else?" I mutter sotto voce.

1:00 p.m. Isaac switches cars and drives with me. Says telephone registrar informed him that my wife couldn't attend today because she had some physical problems. I am amazed at how thorough they were. Mumble something about "difficulty walking," and he drives on. Tells me about leaving Israel, coming to New York, and then to Florida. He's going to play the Jewish card when push comes to shove.

1:15 p.m. The cars head back for lunch!

How do I evaluate a free lunch served at a cemetery? Ambiance, quality, presentation, and service.

First, ambiance. We sit at a conference table and eat under the gazes of previously deceased beings who look down on us from the headstone plaques that adorn the wall—not exactly conducive to eating and digesting food. The decorated paper plates lend a nice touch. Not even a utensil (plastic or otherwise) to mar the atmosphere. No self-respecting Zagat member would ever eat a meal here.

Quality is the next test.

Enter the room first, as the others were still tomb gazing. The only food on the table is a dish of tea sandwiches and a bag of chips. Catch my breath. Am starving and want to dig in (even the mini-sandwiches look appetizing), but Judy had taught me that I shouldn't eat till everyone was seated. The others come in with Kathy, who tells us, "There are three kinds of sandwiches, ham salad, egg salad, and chicken salad."

"Looks good enough to eat!"

Martha offers the sandwich tray to me first. Must look hungry, but defer to her. Then take one of each. Swallow in one bite. The only difference I could tell was in the color—red, white, and yellow. The tuna has more Hellmann's than Bumble Bee. The warm Sprite is a nice touch. Guess someone thought you had to leave the Sprite out to breathe.

When I finish my eighth tea sandwich, Isaac comes in and has a few. It's always a good sign when someone eats his own food. Soon there are only four forlorn-looking wedges left, and everyone is finished. They whisk the "unwanteds" away, probably for the dinner seminar.

As for presentation, I can best sum it up by quoting Kathy's words as she entered. "Looks good enough to eat," she hyperbolizes as she attempts to wipe the egg off her face.

As for service, it's self-service. Kathy and Isaac clean up. Soon we'll be down to the last step in the day's program, the dreaded one-on–one.

1:30 p.m. Meal over, back to business. Isaac gives out "Personal Planning Portfolio," an eighteen-page booklet to list all the important facts about one's bank accounts, brokerage accounts, location of will, and other vital information to help your survivors handle your post-mortem affairs.

Isaac gets fourth phone call and has to excuse himself again. Keithly jokes that "People are dying to get in here." Nervous smiles all around.

1:37 p.m. Isaac gets up and asks Martha and John to join him in another room. Guess he figures they were a better bet than a man here without his wife, even if he were a <u>landsman</u> (Yiddish for "compatriot"). As they get up to leave, I'm reminded of a scene from a gangster movie in which the warden and a priest lead the condemned man out of his cell to the electric chair. Except in the movie the condemned man had a choice of his last meal.

Kathy closes door, faces Keithly and me, and asks, "Any questions?" The minister responds, "What are the costs?" She smiles; she's in her element now. Flips through binder.

"In ground, $2,000 to $4,000," she reports. "Mausoleum, about $9,000. But when you get through with the add-ons for in ground, they cost almost the same." Also says that mausoleums are nice and "airy" and are "clean and with no bugs." My guess is that commission is better on mausoleums.

Offers five-year payment plans. Says plots have doubled in value past eight years. Great investment. Ask if the plots can be sold. She says the cemetery doesn't buy back plots, but she acts as an agent for anyone who wants to sell to an individual. Maybe I should buy a few. Seems safer than the stock market. And if things go sour, I can always crawl into one and die when it's time to have my ticket punched.

"You can save money on a mausoleum," she says, "by squeezing two people into one crypt, if one body is cremated, and the urn is snugged in." Sounds comfy to me. Great for a wife who has always yearned for intimacy.

Kathy mentions she and Isaac can help take care of your funeral arrangements. Says both are licensed by the state.

Kathy mentions she and Isaac can cater your next luncheon. (Just a little joke of mine.)

Asks if have any questions. Try hard to think of a question. Wonder if the smoke from the crematorium causes any problems. I wonder if they only fire them up them at night. Decide not to inquire. "No," I reply lamely, feeling very inadequate. She grimaces. Wipe a trace of mayo off my lips.

Kathy makes last-ditch effort to get my business. Asks me to come back with my wife, because she says no matter how many notes I take, it's not the same as seeing the grounds in person. Tell her I'll speak to Judy as soon as I get home. She smiles faintly. Can see it sounds to her like, "The check is in the mail."

Keithly asks another question. "When a body is made ready for cremation, is it housed in a container?" Kathy responds, "It's put in a container of wood or heavy-duty cardboard." Makes me think of those Bickford quick-start briquette containers. Cringe. Wonder if they use lighter fluid.

Jolted by a recollection of our vacation visit years earlier to the banks of the Ganges at sunrise to watch the funeral pyres light up the brightening sky. The air was acrid.

Am reminded of spending one summer sixty years or so ago at a home a few miles from Sing Sing prison in New York. The story went around that the lights in the homes dimmed whenever there was an electrocution at the prison, but I can't vouch for it. Just want to add a light touch to a subject that might be a bit distressing to some of my readers.

"I don't have a will," Keithly declares. Kathy picks right up on this by offering to give him her brother's card—explaining that he's an attorney and very experienced in this field. Keithly says he'll call.

Keithly seems like a nice man and a serious one, befitting his calling. I can tell he has nowhere to go after this session. "Do you enjoy your work?" he asks. "Yes," Kathy replies, "I feel I have a calling from God to work here." The minister nods in understanding. "It must be hard to be around grieving families all day," he intones. "No, I love my work." she replies earnestly. Guess she thrives on tuna.

"I'm not afraid to die," the minister says, apropos of nothing. Makes me afraid.

Take this as my cue to get up and leave. I thank Kathy for her help and hotfoot it out the door before she has time to detain me.

Wonder how long the minister stayed on.

Wonder if Martha and John put pen to paper and made Isaac's day. Hope so.

MANO A MANO

The printed invitation I received in the mail…
A Personal Lunch or Dinner on Me
at Abe & Louie's Steak Restaurant

…held out the promise of another gourmet adventure. I grabbed the phone, because Abe & Louie's Restaurant is as good as it gets when it comes to steak in Boca. But when the telephone registrar informed me that this offer was for a *two-person seminar*—just Mr. Financial Planner and me—I was completely taken aback. I tried to balance the aroma and melt-in-your-mouth taste of Abe and Louie's steaks against having to sit face to face for an hour with my host. Would I have the nerve to order a tomato and onion salad, sirloin steak, fries, creamed spinach, and cheesecake for dessert, knowing that the chances that I'd hire him as my financial planner were as likely as snow falling on Boca?

I wondered how long it would take him to see through my ploy. I envisioned him deforking me just as I was about to take my first bite. Or worse, would he rise in his chair and denounce me as a freeloader and have me ushered from the dining room steakless?

I examined the smiling but stern face on the invitation and decided that I was no match for him. I told the telephone registrar that I'd have to get back to her. Whew, that was close.

THE EYES HAVE IT

I spied an ad:

LUNCH AND LEARN
THE CATARACT CURE
TUESDAY, JUNE 8, 2010
Complimentary Lunch
Served at 11:30 A.M.
SEMINAR—12 P.M.

The only trouble was that I've already had the cataracts on both of my eyes removed. Since the lunch was to be served first, I wondered if I could eat, get up from the table, go to the bathroom, and then split.

I continued reading the ad:

If you or someone you know suspect
you may have cataracts,
don't miss the lecture.

Since I certainly do *suspect that someone I know* may have cataracts, instead of bolting after lunch, I could look the eye doctor in the eye and say to him in the "Brief Private Evaluation with the Doctor" that was included with the seminar, "I sure do know someone with cataracts, and I'll be glad to give them your card. And by the way, the lunch was great. Just a bit too much pepper on the salad."

A REAL STEAL

As I left my eighth free lunch seminar, I felt as if I had hit a double without even coming up to bat. As you read on, you'll understand my allusion.

Let's start with the engraved invitation I received in the mail a few weeks ago, inviting "me and a guest" to a presentation discussing the stock market. "It's best suited to those between the ages of sixty-five and eighty." I'd have to lie again about my age, but in the interest of self-aggrandizement, I had no choice.

The reward this time was a complimentary gift card for $70 *per couple* to dine at Ruth's Chris Steakhouse. This was a refreshing twist on all the other seminars I had attended, where meals were served at an ung_dly hour and you ate breakfast at 10:00 a.m., lunch at 2:00 p.m., or dinner at 4:00 p.m.

I tried to convince Judy to join me to earn her $35 certificate, but she declined. I'm the only breadwinner in this family, it seems. I wondered if I could pay someone $20 to come with me, and I'd pocket his certificate, for a fast $15 profit.

The day before the seminar, I received the usual call to make sure that I was coming.

On the day of the seminar, I arrived at their offices right at 10:00 a.m.—pretty nice digs and just a few miles away. I was ushered into a large conference room and helped myself to coffee. I said hello to the only other participant in the room. Another couple joined us.

At a quarter past ten a man walked in and said he's sorry to have to tell us that he has to cancel the seminar because not enough people showed up.

I was thunderstruck. Who in their right mind would pass up a free $35 gift card? Perhaps a plague had struck Boca overnight. Perhaps Obama's stimulus program was working after all, and the recession was over, and there was no chance of a double dip.

"But not to worry," he said. "You'll still get your Ruth's Chris gift card." I had to restrain myself from jumping for joy. It would have looked unseemly. I tried to look as disheartened as possible. The other guests kept their feelings under control.

He offered to have us come to a forthcoming seminar that they had scheduled. I wanted to ask him if I would get another gift card for attending, but thought better of it.

I lit out the door clutching my gift card, half expecting to see the streets crowded with people wearing masks to ward off the plague.

The only downside to this bit of luck is that $35 doesn't go very far at Ruth's Chris. I wonder if they add a surcharge for splitting an entrée.

INTERMEZZO #2

I treated the research for this article as seriously as if I were writing a treatise for my PhD. I even explored the discussion in detail in Wikipedia, the free online encyclopedia.

I learned that the phrase "free lunch" refers to a tradition in saloons from about 1870 in the United States of offering free food with the purchase of at least one drink.

The nearly indigent "free-lunch fiend" was a recognized social type. An 1872 New York Times story about "loafers and free-lunch men" who "toil not, yet they 'get along,'…visiting saloons, trying to bum drinks from strangers. He devours whatever he can, and, while the bartender is occupied, tries to escape unnoticed."

"Free lunch" was also a phrase used years ago to describe a meal served on airline flights to passengers flying in coach. That was ages ago, in the days when you could borrow a pillow for a few hours "on the house."

The phrase "There's no such thing as a free lunch" is popularly associated with economist Milton Friedman, who published a book under that title in 1975, but others used the phrase as far back as the 1940s.

I won't bore you with any more trivia on this worthy subject, but I must say that any similarity between Earl Bronsteen and the "free-lunch fiend" described two paragraphs above is purely coincidental.

JOSLYN WITH ONLY A FRINGE ON TOP

I don't know how much latitude I'm allowed in picking subjects for this dissertation on free lunch seminars. One item that sparked my reportorial interest was an ad for T's Lounge, a "gentlemen's club" in West Palm Beach. I concentrated on the words:

FREE DRINK - BRING IN THIS AD AND YOUR SECOND DRINK IS ON US

Bottoms up.

If my research takes me to cemeteries and restaurants in search of a free meal, why not to a gentlemen's club in search of no more than a free drink? I felt it my duty to find out if the club's claim that: "T's Lounge offers all the amenities that you would expect from a true Gentlemen's Club and a highly motivated staff ready to help you_*party all night long*!"

I wondered if there is an age limit. I wondered if they have a defibrillator on the premises. I was sure they had a vibrator. I wondered if I'd have to *party all night long* (like the ad said) or whether I could party just once.

I wondered if my soon-to-be new friend, Joslyn James, the dancer pictured in the ad, knows CPR.

I leave it to you to wonder what happened when I checked out T's lounge. I will say that rumors that I got up on the stage and danced are exaggerated.

PS. In the interest of transparency I have to admit to being a teetotaler.

PPS. I included this episode upon the suggestion of a friend who advised me that, "You can't sell a book today that doesn't have explicit sexual content. The more graphic the prose, the better it flows."

Well, dear reader, this is as prurient as this book gets. If this doesn't satisfy your licentious desires, I suggest you call 561-471-9530 (see ad) and make a reservation. Tell Joslyn that you're a friend of mine, and she'll take good care of you. If at first she doesn't recognize my name, remind her that after our first lap dance she called me "Swifty."

THE FREE LUNCH COST $82.66

The $35 gift card for Ruth's Chris Steak House that I received from the aborted seminar a while ago was burning a hole in my pocket. At my age I don't like to let gift cards remain unused too long, like the old saw about never buying green bananas. I knew the $35 credit probably wouldn't even cover the price of a steak for one, but I decided to take the bull by the horns and make reservations for the two of us.

I went online to "Open Table" to book our reservation—not that you need a reservation during the height of summer in Boca Raton, but because I get a $1 credit for each one I book. This will help offset the $2 tip for valet parking.

Judy was excited when I told her we were going to Ruth's Chris that Saturday night. She loves to get dressed up, and she savors steak.

We arrived at 6:30 p.m. As I surveyed the nearly filled room, it was obvious that Judy was the prettiest woman in the room and the best dressed.

The waiter (Tim) got off on my wrong side by asking if we wanted sparkling water or bottled water. He flinched imperceptibly when I told him Boca water would do just fine. However, Judy got into the swim of things by ordering a glass of wine. I splurged on iced tea. A rapid mental mathematical calculation indicated that almost half of the gift card had already gone up in smoke.

When the drinks came, we toasted the financial planning company that had provided the gift card. Judy smiled. I tried to smile. I saw people at other tables clinking glasses, and I assumed they were here with gift cards from the same financial planner. I waved to them. The wave was unreturned.

Judy ordered the petit filet. The waiter said the larger filet was a much better deal, and implied that the petit filet at six ounces ($32) was half the size of the eight-ounce filet ($39). Judy stuck to her guns. The waiter had lost his second skirmish with us and was getting antsy. We (Judy and I, not Tim and I) split a very good salad and two sides. I was tired of eating steak and ordered crab cakes. Big mistake.

The waiter told us to be careful not to touch the plates, as they were heated to five hundred degrees. We dug in. Judy passed the creamed spinach. It was lukewarm. I mentioned this to Judy, but she didn't make any comment. Just then the manager came by and asked, "How is everything?" I was faced with Dilemma #1 for the evening. I looked at Judy and could tell by her look, and by past experience, that my answer should be, "Fine." He smiled and moved on.

I took another bite of the cooling spinach and called the waiter over and mentioned the offending dish. He gladly offered to replace the item, and did so.

Just to make conversation I asked Judy how her steak compared to the one she had at Outback Steakhouse for about half the price. "They're about the same," she replied. I was flabbergasted. She said her filet tasted as if it had been prepared with a meat tenderizer. I felt down in the mouth, and she could see it on my face. "I wasn't going to say anything, because I didn't want to spoil your dinner," she said. "You should have sent it back immediately," I answered.

The manager came near, and I brought the situation to his attention. He could not have been nicer and told Judy that she should have mentioned it earlier and that he would have replaced it and that he was very sorry.

The waiter returned and told us that the manager offered us a free dessert ($8.75) as recompense. Judy didn't want to accept and here was my Dilemma #2. "Should I go against Judy's wishes to keep a low profile and not seem to be a complainer, or should I have the bread pudding, my favorite dessert? I compromised by ordering it to go.

I added this doggie bag to the one for Kittles—the third crab cake that I didn't eat, and after Judy's coffee and payment of the balance of $82.66, we left the restaurant. I restrained myself and didn't carp about the crab.

The unsavory steak had put a damper on the evening, and now I was faced with Dilemma #3. As I handed the valet my parking chit, he asked, "How was everything?" I wondered if I told him about our problems with the steak and spinach if he would refund my $2 tip, but Judy was standing right next to me, so I said, "Fine." I could see she was pleased. The valet couldn't have cared less.

I had my phone with me, and a passing stranger was good enough to take our photo to commemorate the evening. I wondered if I should make an attempt to sell him the crab cake and bread pudding in my doggy bag to try to recoup some of the $82.66, but I knew I'd have to sleep alone for a week if I did.

PS. My dictionary describes a moral as a short, precise rule, usually written in a rather literary style as the conclusion to the story, used to help people remember the best or most sensible way to behave.

I pondered what the moral of this story was. Was it:

1. If you go out to a fine restaurant and the food is not to your liking, you should never mention it to your spouse, the manager, the waiter, or even the parking valet.

2. If you go out to a fine restaurant and the food is not to your liking, you should immediately mention it to your spouse and/or the manager, waiter, or parking valet.

3. If you never go to a fine restaurant, you will never be disappointed.

THE DOG DAYS OF SUMMER

I've had to enlist my friends' help in finding free lunch opportunities in the midst of summer here in steamy South Florida. At the beginning of August, all my calendar showed for the foreseeable future were two breakfasts at memorial parks—talk of scraping the bottom of the crypt. My goal of getting at least one free meal a week had gone up in smoke.

When I received a letter from Loren, I knew it contained an invite, as he is one of my seminar scouts. The heading of the ad he sent seemed promising enough:

DON'T MISS THIS FREE SEMINAR
BREAKFAST WILL BE SERVED

And since JP Morgan Chase sponsored the seminar, I was sure they wouldn't serve anything less than pitchers of fresh orange juice, piles of pancakes, mounds of muffins, and carafes of coffee. Jamie Dimon wouldn't do any less.

The seminar was scheduled for 7:30–10:00 a.m. So far, so good.

You, my reader, know there's going to be a fly in my blueberry pancakes. Yes, as I read on, I learned that the seminar was to be held in Miami, at least an hour's drive from my home, without taking into account rush-hour traffic. I'd have to get up before the crack of dawn.

I wondered if I should call up Jamie Dimon and ask him how late I could show up and still get the free breakfast. I wondered if I should ask him if he planned any dinner seminars. I bet the pancakes would be lousy. I threw the ad away.

BENEDICT ARNOLD

I felt a little like Benedict Arnold when I called to make a reservation for a free dinner seminar at Ruth's Chris Steak House. That's because it was less than a month ago that I had enjoyed a medium-rare filet mignon at Ruth Chris's courtesy of the same firm (but different office) that had just mailed me an invitation to a free dinner seminar. Last month I traveled to West Palm Beach for my repast. A local branch of the same company was sponsoring another seminar, which was to be held in my backyard in Boca Raton.

I was not sure if the sponsor, a fairly large accounting firm and financial planner, kept records of prior registrants (freeloaders). I decided to take my chances, lifted the phone, and called to place my registration request. The telephone registrar didn't recognize my voice. I had taken the precaution of speaking through a handkerchief. So far, so good.

When I gave her my name, I expected a buzzer to go off, but nothing happened. She took down all my pertinent information and said she'd send me an e-mail confirmation.

I don't want to sound like Chicken Little. The worst thing that could happen would be that I'd have to sit through the sixty-minute harangue and then at 4:00 p.m., just as the waiters started to bring in the dinner, the moderator would unmask me, in front of a dozen or so strangers. I'd still be able to make it home in time to eat. I can't wait till July 20.

Fast forward to August 19. I received a call in the morning from a representative of the sponsor of the dinner. (Yes, this is the firm the SEC slammed.) He informed me that in checking their records, he found that I had previously attended one of their seminars in Palm Beach. I told him that indeed I had, but that I hadn't felt any rapport with the speaker. The friendly voice told me that the seminar he was going to run tomorrow would be different and invited me to attend. I agreed to be there.

I was torn. Should I take more than one free steak dinner from the same firm? What an ethical problem. On the one hand, I felt I should go, because if I had brought my wife the sponsor would be on the hook for two steak dinners. On the other hand, what if one of my eight grandchildren happened to read these essays and found out that I had double dipped? I wanted to write a letter to the ethicist who writes for *The New York Times* and put the query to him, but I didn't have enough time. Later that afternoon I became chickenhearted. I called and cancelled.

A month later I received a third invitation from the same company. The invite convinced me that they really wanted me to come to their next seminar and to enjoy a second filet mignon on the house. It was apparent that they were willing to take their chances that their Boca Raton office's spokesman would make a more convincing presentation than the one in West Palm Beach.

This was my third complimentary visit to Ruth's Chris Steak House in the past two months, and I began to feel like a regular. I arrived at 2:50 p.m. and found a parking spot in a free lot nearby. My good fortune continued once I stepped through the doors of one of Boca's finest beef emporiums. A hostess ushered me through the empty and darkened restaurant to a private dining room in the back of the mahogany and leather chophouse.

3:00 p.m. "Hi, I'm Jane," says the welcoming, outstretched hand. It is connected to a slim body encased in a businesslike black dress topped by a pleasant face and warm smile. (Late twenties, I would guess.) "Take any seat," she says.

Sit down at an empty table in a chair facing the ever-present projector and screen. Two tables set up to serve six people and one table for two are shoehorned into the small, dark-paneled room. Waiter asks what I'd like to drink and fills my glass with a Floridian's favorite summer drink, iced tea. Second bit of good fortune concerns the waiter. As luck would have it, he just happens to be the same man who served Judy and me on prior visit. You probably don't recall, but I related that he was very officious on that occasion and that because of his attitude, I left a smaller tip than usual. Fortunately, doesn't recognize me—at least don't think he does. To make sure he doesn't poison my food, plan to ask a dinner partner to be my official taster.

Third bit of fortune was that speaker doesn't recognize my name as the person he had spoken to over the phone about coming to a second seminar. You probably don't remember, but he invited me to attend, because he was sure his presentation would convince me to utilize his services. I was sure he'd pressure me because he had something to prove and since I was a second-timer.

3:05 p.m. We (three couples, three women, and another man) open packets of materials and, at suggestion of waiter, examine menu: choice of small filet mignon, crab cakes, or chicken breast. No contest. Ten guests order filet and one orders crab cakes. Entrée was to be preceded by a Caesar salad and followed by nothing.

Lunchmate is a grey-haired, craggy-faced, amiable man dressed in khaki shorts, a polo shirt and well-worn sneakers. I assume he's single or that his wife is having an affair and couldn't care less how "hubby" dressed for dinner at Ruth's Chris. I ask him if he often goes to seminars. Replies, "No, but I was attracted by name Ruth's Chris." From his dress figure he's another freeloader and take instant liking to him. Maybe I'll get his phone number and have Judy invite him and his all-forgiving wife for dinner (Dutch, of course).

3:10 p.m. Jane announces speaker was held up at office, but he'll arrive shortly.

3:15 p.m. James, a neatly dressed young man in his thirties, enters. Apologizes for being late and turns on PowerPoint projector. Asks us to fill out info form in our packet. Says he needs this material so his office can cross check to see if someone tries to sneak into more than one luncheon. Hold my breath, but the sky doesn't fall.

James refers to the three empty chairs, which he says will be filled by latecomers. (They never show. Must have died, or else how can you account for passing up Ruth's free filet?) Tells us that they usually have many more people at these seminars, but sparse turnout must be due to the Jewish holidays and the summer season.

He then lets us know about his background. Buffalo born, bred, and raised. Educated as a CPA. Worked for firm for five years when they offered him the opportunity to transfer to their Boca Raton office. "No brainer," he says, "Gladly willing to leave Buffalo's harsh winters." James and his girlfriend, the very same Jane, have been here a little over a year. I wonder why they aren't married. Bet Jane wonders the same. But anyone who wants to marry an accountant must have plenty of her own problems.

For the next hour he describes his accounting and money man-agement company and the services they provide. I'll spare you the details, except to relate two brief anecdotes. One time when he is try-ing to bring a point home to us (one I can't recall), he asks audience, "Who is the first person you see when you go into your doctor's office?" Woman raises her hand and shouts, "The receptionist!" James is taken aback. Correct answer was "the nurse." Her response ruins story.

Speaker then follows up with another tale about a client who came to his office for help with his investment portfolio.

"The man was single, had $500,000 to invest, and didn't have any children," the lecturer discloses.

"What's his name?" same woman interjects, half jokingly.

4:15 p.m. He's been talking for an hour and hasn't finished presentation. "Do you mind if we go past our time schedule by ten minutes?" he inquires. Before I get the chance to tell him that, "I do mind and let's get on with our dinner," my sneakered tablemate says, "Go right ahead."

4:40: p.m. Just as I suspected, overtime period becomes extended by twenty-five minutes. In response to query as to how small an account they would take for financial planning, speaker says, "There is no minimum." Goes on to define "no minimum": "Fifty thousand dollars would be OK to open an account, but ten thousand would be too small."

Engage my tablemate in conversation as we await our salad. Turns out he lives in nearby gated community with golf, tennis, and all the amenities. His portfolio is 90 percent municipal bonds yielding a little over 5 percent. That means he has to have at least $2 million in bonds to pay for upkeep on home, country club dues, and everyday living expenses. Tells me he was an accountant and used to work for the IRS as a tax examiner; then, after retiring, he just manages his investments and plays golf. Wonder how a civil servant was able to accumulate that kind of a fortune. Assume he won the lottery and let it go at that. This tale proves you can never tell a man's bank account by the kind of sneakers he wears.

4:50 p.m. Steak arrives on a plate heated to five hundred degrees. Strange to think I could be ravenously hungry at this early hour. Finish the perfectly cooked steak in a few mouthfuls and top it off with few spoonfuls of mashed potatoes and creamed spinach. Woman who ordered crab cakes calls the waiter over to tell him they taste fishy. She gets tartar sauce and lemon to drown out the unpleasant flavor. Maybe the crabs were drenched in oil courtesy of BP.

Almost all the participants sign up for "Complimentary One-Hour Appointment" to review prior tax returns. Avoid setting up appointment, and since speaker is in a hurry to meet a client at his office, he doesn't press the issue.

Another notch in my belt. It's the good life.

SARTORIAL SPLENDOR

"Fix your socks," Judy shouted at me as I headed for the door on my way to a 10:00 a.m. breakfast seminar at a nearby chapel/memorial park. It was raining, and all my wife was worried about was the impression my uneven white tennis socks would make on the rabbi. "It's a reform chapel," I replied. "Anything goes."

I never got to find out what the rabbi thought abut my socks, because he was tied up with a funeral, and the pre-breakfast prayer at the funeral home was delivered by a layman. No one seemed to mind. But I'm a little ahead of myself. Here's my transcript of the notes of the next two hours:

10:00 a.m. Short drive. Been there several times for funerals. Enter large room filled with six spacious round tables. Handshake. Smile. Sign in. Assigned to table #5. Nametagged. Meet Stan, our table's licensed pre-need counselor. Greet tablemates. Examine table—coffee, small plastic cups, OJ in pitcher (not fresh), milk, plastic knife and fork wrapped in paper napkin and bound with rubber band, sliced tomatoes, sliced onions, plus cream cheese in plastic dish. My heart leaps—if there's cream cheese, tomatoes, and onions (as sure as Moses led our people out of bondage in Egypt eons ago), there must be Nova Scotia salmon and bagels in Boca Raton this morning.

Stan interrupts my reverie. Asks each of us (one couple, one other man, and two women) for our addresses and phone numbers. I consider giving false name, but what if he asks for my ID?

10:15 a.m. Speaker turns on mike in front of room and welcomes us. Announces that everyone who signed up for seminar came. Says applaud yourselves. We do lustily. Tells us food will be served in a moment, but please do not eat till prayer is given. Heavyset woman brings in paper plates wrapped in plastic, and each contains bagel, Nova Scotia salmon, and one-half Danish. I'm beside myself. My favorite of favorite breakfasts, and even though I just had my first breakfast two hours ago, I'm dying to dig in. But still no prayer. Reach for coffee pitcher. Woman on my left puts her hand on mine and keeps me from pouring. "Wait," she says. I feel at home.

Speaker intones prayer in Hebrew. I know many of the words. Woman removes her hand from my sleeve, and I know I'm free to enjoy. Slather cream cheese on bagel bedecked with gloriously pink Nova. Delicious—as good as Zabar's. Others add tomatoes and onion. Feeding frenzy. "Nice little breakfast," Stan says proudly. He can taste a sale coming; who wouldn't be dying to sign up after such a feast.

Stan interrogates each of us in between our swallows. Wants to find out if we have a funeral plot, and for those of us who are here alone, if we are married. Woman with strange hairdo says her husband died three years ago. "I was his fourth wife, and he's buried in Chicago with his first wife," she answers matter-of-factly. "We had three good years together," she adds. I guessed that he had a better time with his first wife. Wonder what kind of hairdo first wife sported.

Sylvia announces she's not married. "All a man wants is someone to cook for him and clean up." Surmise her husband committed suicide. She picks up a sliver of onion with her fingers and puts it in her mouth. Bet she wouldn't mind, as Judy does, if I chew my cream-cheesed bagel with my mouth open.

Taking notes at a furious pace. Stan looks over and quizzes me why I've been scribbling away ever since I sat down. Tell him that I have a poor memory. He takes one look at me and doesn't doubt it for a moment. Volunteers come in to clear away plates and dishes. Sylvia notices that Stan has a little Nova left on his plate and asks if she can have the scrap that's left. He nods; she grabs. Too full to eat my Danish and wrap it up in plastic for a mid-afternoon snack. Wouldn't give mine to Sylvia in a million years.

10:30 a.m. Topic of seminar is "The importance of planning your funeral arrangements in advance" so that, "...when a death occurs, the survivors are left with little more to do than decide when the service should be held." He also says that by planning in advance, the family saves money because it avoids "emotional overspending." Says at time of death family members may react by saying, "Nothing is too good for my spouse/parent," or "If I don't spend a lot of money on the funeral and casket, people will think I didn't care." Says people who pre-plan save an average of $900 per funeral. Sounds good to everyone at my table but Sylvia, who couldn't care less; she's not spending a penny on any man, dead or alive. Speaker says his funeral home has handled thirty thousand funerals. Wonder how many of them had enjoyed a free breakfast seminar beforehand. That's what I call pre-planning. Discloses prices are discounted if sign up by September 30, and payment can be made on the installment plan without interest. Stan can help families buy monuments and cemetery plots. Full-service shop.

One man at another table dozes off, but he doesn't snore. He has a five o'clock shadow. Wonder if he is still there from yesterday's seminar.

I learn: rabbis charge $500 for funeral; some reform rabbis perform funerals with cremation; cost of monuments has come down as they became more popular and more and bigger ones were built; veterans can die for free at beautiful Arlington-like VA cemetery only *fifteen minutes away—plot for two included and monument and internment—save $12,000, but still need casket, rabbi, etc. Speaker tries to downplay VA burial because he says the odds are you won't be buried next to someone Jewish. Woman sitting next to me asks if this means that in the two-person plot you might be buried with someone other than your husband. She really did ask this, and she was quite relieved to learn the truth. Her husband pales.*

11:10 a.m. "Any questions?" speaker asks. Then answers all easily, but no one can get any idea of how much it all costs. That's what he says Stan (and his counterparts at each of the other tables) is there for and now it's "appointment time." Stan takes out his calendar book, and just as he turns to me, the guest sitting opposite asks him a question. Jump up and start to leave. Stan looks as if he wants to tackle me, but I put out my hand as a straight-arm and he lets me by.

11:30 p. m. Hit the parking lot at a full trot and look back to see if Stan is chasing me. Start up car with Danish stuffed in my pocket, for later.

PS. A month later I called Stan, the family counselor at our table, and told him that I had come to the seminar only because I was writing a series of articles about free lunch seminars. He remembered that I had been taking a lot of notes. I told him it was not an expose, just an autobiographical account. I asked if he would be willing to be interviewed so that I could learn what it's like on the other side of the table. He said he'd have to ask his boss. Unfortunately, so far he hasn't called back. Too bad. I thought he'd have a lot of interesting stories to tell as a counterpoint to my experiences. Maybe I should have offered to treat him to lunch. That'll be the day.

A CAPITAL INVITATION

The Capital Grille is one of Boca's finest steak restaurants.

Morgan Stanley Smith Barney wants me to join them for lunch there on August 18, 2010.

Topic: Long-term health care

We're booked on a plane to New York that very day.

Can't postpone trip. Paid for tickets.

I went to the Web to look up the restaurant:

"Amazing food, amazing service"—opentable.com.

"Nice venue, great steak and beautiful atmosphere."

"Enjoy quality prime dry aged steaks in an upscale clubby environment"—zagat.com.

"Excellent food. Nice atmosphere"—tripadvisor.com.

The restaurant's Web site trumpeted:

"Every now and then, life calls for fine cuisine. At the Capital Grille, it is our great pleasure to prepare for you what we humbly suggest might be among the finest.

Choose from critically acclaimed dry aged steaks, hand-carved and grilled to perfection, a variety of seafood flown in fresh from both shores and unique daily culinary offerings crafted with fresh, local, *artisanal* ingredients."

I don't know what artisanal ingredients are, but I'd be willing to try anything once.

MEDIUM-RARE DOUBLEHEADER

The morning of August 10, 2010, was cloudy and rainy. Not an auspicious start for my steak doubleheader at two of Boca's finest restaurants.

I worked at my computer till 10:00 a.m. Then it's morning naptime, but I was so excited, I tossed and turned and never fell asleep. I won't be as sharp as usual without my hour's rest. I drove to Abe & Louie's Restaurant. I hoped to get there early enough to avoid complimentary valet parking. I pulled into an empty lot, but parked facing the man working at the valet's booth. He looked daggers at me as I turned off the engine. I'm going to have to walk past him to get into the restaurant. No way to dig a tunnel without shovel.

I looked around to see who else going into the restaurant might also be a freeloader and was surprised to see my friend Herb, the guy I took to my first free lunch seminar at The Cheesecake Factory. He told me one of his friends invited him to Abe & Louie's to join him for the seminar. I can see Herb's a professional guest, and I doubt he'll feel he has to reciprocate for the free lunch I got for him weeks earlier.

12:00 a.m. Enter back room set up with five tables of four settings and a main table in front. Sit with Herb, his host, and another friend. Room full, everyone well dressed (Judy would approve).

Sit down. Steak knife sits atop my white napkin. Augurs well.

Grab menu. No steak in sight. Flummoxed. I read on:

CHOICE OF: "Abe's cheeseburger," wood-grilled chicken breast, roasted turkey club sandwich, and two salads. Plus cake for dessert.

Stare at steak knife. Feel like plunging it into Abe or Louis. Order burger, medium, and cheesecake. Can't win them all. Still have tonight's meal at Morton's to salvage my presumed Red-Letter Day.

Waiter brings iced tea for all and passes platters of bruschetta and chicken on a stick with a flourish. Nice touch, but doesn't make up for the absence of steak.

Suit and tie (Joey) joins table and sits down next to Herb. Handshakes. Smiles. He's with the Wall Street firm promoting the lunch. Exchange pleasantries. Resident of Boca via the Bronx. Men at table perk up at the mention of Jerome Avenue.

12:20 p.m. Speaker welcomes everyone. Introduces man from Pimco (biggest bond fund in world), whose company is paying for the lunch. Pimco is a cheapskate in my book. Who ever heard of going to Abe & Louie's for a hamburger?

Speech continues:

Topic is "Goals For Today," which he says are:

1. Have a great meal.

2. Gain at least two insightful pieces of knowledge.

3. Schedule a follow-up conversation.

My goal in only numero uno.

12:42 p.m. Lunch is served. Double whammy. Burger is well done, not medium. Could have done as well at Burger King. Even worse is that my neighbor on the left is eating sliced steak (medium) adorned with thick slices of juicy red tomatoes. I conjecture that he has ordered off the menu, but that seems unlikely. Ask for menu. Sure enough, there it was. I was so groggy from not having had my morning nap that I misread the item he had ordered as just a tomato and onion salad—my tired eyes missed the word steak.

Ask him how he enjoyed his steak. He said it was great. Utter four-letter word under my breath. Tell Herb that I really goofed. Man on left hears me say how much I love tomatoes. He has one tomato slice left and puts it on my plate. Shake his hand. Then he takes some of my fries in exchange. Good trade. Wish he had traded some of his steak for my well-done burger.

Gets worse. Get my "just desserts." Ordered the cheesecake. It's one-third the size of the chocolate seven-layer cake.

1:10 p.m. Speeches abound. Like some of the things they say. Two people at my table seem particularly interested in going forward with Oppenheimer's people. Write on guest's info sheet, "Call me."

Decide to try men's room. Very masculine. Not as nice as at Ruth's Chris. Muzak—music to pee by.

1:40 p.m. Ask Herb to take my picture. Suit asks, "Why are you having your picture taken?" Then he answers his own question, "So you can prove to your wife where you went all dressed up." Everyone laughs.

I rushed home to type up my notes before I had to leave for Morton's. Porterhouse tonight, or bust. I felt a bit shaky as I entered my car, nap-deprived. I drove to the wrong shopping center even though I've been to the Town Center home of Morton's hundreds of times. I turned around and retraced my steps. I wondered if they would hold my spot if I'm late. I wondered about Alzheimer's.

4:05 p.m. Sign in. Receptionist tells me that everyone who signed up came, and two people arrived without having signed up. Large wood-paneled room. Sixty to seventy people. Sit with friendly couple.

Now can relax. No silverware. Don't recognize anyone from any of the previous eight seminars I've attended.

4:12 p.m. Bill, our speaker, takes microphone. Large man dressed in nondescript slacks and a floral shirt sticking out over his rotund belly. States that Morton's has another group coming in to use half of the room at 6:00 p.m., so the attendees in the front will then have to get up and go across the street to Wendy's for dinner. He laughs; guests laugh nervously. "No," he says. "You'll be eating in the main dining room." People relax. He should know there are some things you don't kid about.

Subject of seminar is "How and Why to Convert Your IRA to a Roth IRA." Info packet contains sheet with "Six Rules For The Event":

1. Please be respectful of our staff and Morton's staff.

2. No foul language.

3. No debates with me. If you disagree, "cool it."

4–6. Info about making appointments.

He must be used to some tough, belligerent audiences. I look around. Seniors as far as the eye can see. Not a biker in the crowd. Wonder what could be so inflammatory about IRAs.

For the next ninety minutes or so he explains how to save on income and estate taxes. Promotes annuities as the way to fund customer's taxes on conversion. He refers to one new annuity as, "Almost too good to be true." I agree.

His speech is salted (kosher) with Jewish phrases. Speaks in a haimish (homespun) manner. He's a maven (expert) when it comes to individual retirement accounts. Says, "Don't be a meshuggener (crazy person), switch your IRA to a Roth. (Wonder if he is recommending a switch to Roth because Roth is Jewish.) Half of his audience understands the references. The subject is very technical. Try to follow, but in my bleary sleep-deprived state, it's all a blur. Come awake when he gives some tax examples to prove his thesis, and his math and mine don't agree. Who cares? Certainly not the kvetching (complaining) women in sleeveless blouses who are freezing. Bill sends associate to get AC turned off. Then continues his sales pitch.

5:45 p.m. Bill ends it. Will collect appointment forms at dinner. Doesn't mind if we are not going to set up meeting; prefers that to our setting up a date and then canceling (that's what I was going to do).

We move into main dining room. Ambience all around. Grab seat at head of a table for ten people. Steak knife shines brightly. Déjà vu.

Start conversation with eightyish woman on my right who came without her husband. "How'd you like the seminar?" I ask. "Well," she answers, "a man getting up to speak in front of an audience shouldn't dress like a schlump." I laugh. "That's just what my wife would say," I respond. "That's what any wife would say," woman on my other side retorts.

Chat with her eightyish husband. Retired endodontist from Pennsylvania. Ask him if he knows my endodontist. He doesn't. Nothing else to talk about. Nice teeth.

Neatly dressed waiter comes to take our order. "Chicken or filet?" he inquires. At last I'm going to be rewarded for my efforts. "Pink center," I say. One woman asks how the chicken is prepared. Is she kidding? This ain't Chick-fil-A.

6:00 p.m. Serve Caesar salad. Nothing special. Woman asks if she can have a different salad. "No." he responds. Et tu, Brute?

Iced tea served.

Three people at my table order a glass of red wine a la carte. I'm impressed, certainly not freeloaders. They travel in different circles. Most people do.

6:15 p.m. Butter dish placed on table.

Schlump's assistant comes around to each person to try to arrange appointments for one-on-one interviews at their office. They respond:

"I'm going on vacation."

"I have to speak to my CPA."

"I have to speak to my husband."

"I'm not ready yet."

The assistant has heard all this before and persistently tries to get people to commit to a specific date. No success at our table. Think most people overwhelmed with all the information presented. Tough to digest on an empty stomach.

6:20 p.m. Bread arrives.

6:30 p.m. Filet follows. Melts in mouth, but too rare. Wonder if should eat some more and then send it back. Decide to tough it out.

Side of steamed fresh broccoli is the biggest, most colorful portion I have ever seen, but tasteless. Have to dump béarnaise on broccoli to flavor it.

If you tilt your head 45 degrees to the left and stare at this photo you'll be able to make out a face—two eyes, nose, and mouth. The mashed potatoes look like a rabbit sitting down looking backwards.

Dinner companion on my left asks for doggie bag. My kind of man. It was his wife who ordered a glass of wine. Typical Boca couple.

6:55 p.m. Small slice of cheesecake. Too tired to eat more than a bite. Skip coffee. Skip out.

I checked out the bathroom (Muzak resounds off the marble). Every expensive steak house has Muzak. Wonder which restaurant will be the first to have a three-piece mariachi band playing next to the urinals. I'd like to be there for the ribbon cutting. Bet for the ribbon they use two-ply toilet paper.

My free lunch seminar doubleheader is history. Gluttony pays.

I get home and fall into bed. I'm so tired I have trouble falling asleep. Decide to count cows. It works.

INTERMEZZO #2

Perhaps you're wondering how I got started in my life of crime. Well, perhaps the word crime is too harsh for my frequent lunchtime forays into the pocketbooks of the wealthy (using Obama's definition of the wealthy, anyone who makes over $250,000). My cavalier approach to dining out will most often not cost my hosts a dime, as they usually have to guarantee a certain fixed dollar amount is spent—and there are always plenty of no-shows. And there is always the possibility that I might wind up a client if the presentation "rings my bell," as it has twice so far for big bucks.

My first nefarious deed took place when I was about eight or nine. We lived in Belle Harbor, Long Island, having moved there when I was four from my birthplace, Brooklyn. I was a great baseball fan, and collecting baseball cards was my passion. Mel Ott, Carl Hubbell, and Lefty O'Doul were my heroes. Those were the days when the Giants played where the belonged, at the Polo Grounds in Harlem, and their archrivals, the Brooklyn Dodgers, had the good sense to reside on Flatbush Avenue.

My parents gave me a small weekly allowance, and I used most of it to buy packs of baseball cards, containing five cards and bubble gum. The objective was to acquire a complete set of a few hundred stars. We traded cards with one another, dealing away our extras in exchange for ones we were missing.

The boys in our group used to "flip cards" to try to increase their collection. One boy would flip a card to the floor (it would turn over and over till it wound up on the floor as a "heads" (picture side up) or as "tails" (the backside containing statistics). His adversary would flip one of his cards, and if he matched the card on the floor, he won both. I considered myself quite a good flipper in those days, not so much anymore.

One fateful day my best friend came over to flip cards. I can still remember standing in a room in the back of our house and starting the contest with Marty Fields. For some reason I had lost my touch, and soon, along with it, my entire collection of prized baseball cards (even Mel Ott's).

It was the second worst day of my tender years, the first being when Sparky ran away. I was inconsolable. I couldn't share my loss with anyone because I was so embarrassed.

How could I tell the ebullient red-haired Annette Kaplan that I was a loser? What would the dark-tressed Carolyn Mass think of me? I wanted them to always remember me as someone who was very good at playing Doctor.

My allowance was so small it would take a year to rebuild my collection and my image as the leader of our group. I was even too ashamed to take part in our regular coed game of Doctor.

The local candy store sold baseball cards. One day I went into the store, with a loose-fitting sweater over my shirt, and furtively stuffed a handful of baseball cards under my sweater. I went up to the counter to pay for the one pack of cards I held out in my hand. I guess I looked a little young to be pregnant. The owner accosted my sweater and me. I ran home crying and swore never to wear that sweater again.

My relationship with Marty suffered after he won all my cards. Shortly thereafter we moved to Manhattan, because my father, a

CPA, found the commute to his office in the city too arduous, especially during tax season. I never saw Marty until some fifty years
later when I ran into him on a train commuting to Manhattan.
He had followed in his father's footsteps and was a dentist with
offices on Wall Street. I had also followed into my father's practice
(accounting), but left it ten years later to seek fame and fortune on
Wall Street.

One day I got a toothache while at work and called Marty. He
told me to come right over. He did a lot of drilling, but didn't wait
until the Novocain had taken its full effect. It seemed apparent that
he was getting back at me for abandoning him when we moved
away. I never went back to his office and never saw him again.

I also never saw Annette or Carolyn again. I got better at playing Doctor when I was older. Ask Judy.

I'd like to be able to say that I learned my lesson from my
first criminal experience, but In all honesty I can't. Fast-forward
to 1943. The war was on. I became a forger. I had to. How did I
ever let myself go over the line? Well, I was only seventeen.
Gimme a break!

I was still at college because I was underage. I was playing on
the varsity basketball team at Yale, and one of the prerequisites for
participating was to pass a series of physical fitness tests. The head
of athletics was determined to have all of Yale's student body in
top physical shape, as they would soon be off to war.

Each student had to successfully pass seven different physical
tests if he wanted to participate in varsity athletics. One of them
was to climb a rope that was attached to a ceiling twenty feet
above the ground. While I always excelled at sports, my arms were
weak, and there was no way in the world that I could climb that
high. Fortunately for me, we carried our own scorecards. I initialed
the box for this test indicating I had passed. I felt no guilt.

The other test I couldn't pass was being able to run a mile in a certain number of minutes. I was a sprinter, but not a distance runner. My pencil went to work and "Voila!" I passed.

I hope there aren't any children reading these confessions, because they may come away with the feeling that crime does pay. Just tell them to become investment bankers, and they won't have any ethical problems to worry about.

Now imagine it's 1944. I was in the Army Air Force and stationed at Scott Field outside of St. Louis. This time I committed a real indiscretion, going AWOL. I wound up in the guardhouse wearing loose-fitting prison stripes, but not for going AWOL—listen up.

My best friend was Bob Bruton, from Churchville, New York. He was a devil-may-care kind of guy, and one day he said, "We have nothing to do this weekend, and we're not eligible to receive a pass to leave the base, so let's go over the fence." The fence part comes in later. The two of us followed a railroad track that ran into the base; it was unguarded, as there was a mile of track to traverse to get to the main road outside of camp.

We hitched a ride to the local racetrack and spent the day gambling on the ponies. All the fresh air left us hungry. I remember Bob saying, "I'm so hungry I could eat a horse." We stopped at a roadside diner, and he probably did. (Even so, it was better than Army food.) Afterward we headed back toward the base. We bummed a ride back to camp and got out a short distance from the gate, which was patrolled by MPs. (It was too dark to attempt to walk the mile of unlit railroad track.) The lights around the gate were so bright, it was almost like daylight, but somehow we were able to crawl unseen on our stomachs the one hundred or so yards and sneak under the fence—no worse for wear for our day's exploits.

Another Army malfeasance occurred one evening when I went into town with two buddies (dressed in our Air Force uniforms) to "hit" the bars and look for girls. St. Louis was, and still is, known as the city of beer. For us, it was never the city of girls.

Only 3.2 beer was served, but one of my friends, Bill Doniger, a fine Irish lad, made up for the low alcohol content by drinking non-stop. Around midnight we decided to hitchhike back to camp and got a lift part way back to Belleville (which was oft perceptively referred to as the a_ _ hole of America).

After thanking the man who had driven us this far, we got out and raised our thumbs again. But this time we weren't having any success getting a ride. Bill yelled (cursed) at the cars that wouldn't stop for us. Then we heard a police whistle from about a hundred yards down the poorly lit block. A cop shouted to us to keep quiet. Bill took this as a personal affront and ran down to where the cop was standing, leaving us by the road. The next thing we saw was the cop raising his nightstick, whacking Bill on the head, and pushing him into a police car. George and I ran down the street and asked where they were taking him. They gave us the address of the police station, and we grabbed a cab.

When we knocked on the door of the police station, a big, pot-bellied cop wearing a stained white undershirt asked what we wanted. We answered we wanted to testify for our friend. Fatso ordered his assistant to, "Lock them up." We spent the night in a cockroach-infested cell sleeping on metal-slotted cots without mattresses. War is hell.

In the morning the military police came and took the three of us to the prison at Scott Field Army Air Force Base. We were given prison uniforms and spent the next few days in jail. The best part was marching back and forth to the mess hall under the constant gaze of armed guards, with our friends laughing as we went past.

Then, since our training classes were about to start, and the war was more important than anything, we were released.

I never got a good conduct medal, and if I had been caught by the MPs in my next misadventure, I would have been back in the brig. Let me step back in time to introduce this episode.

World War II started for the US in 1942. I was only sixteen and in college, so I was not personally affected. On my eighteenth birthday I enlisted, hoping to become an Air Force pilot. I had just seen a play on Broadway, *Winged Victory*, and in it the pilots killed all the Japanese and got all the girls.

The best-laid plans (and my plans to get laid) went astray. By the time I got into the army, it was 1944, and there was an excess of pilots, but I did get to fly, three hundred hours worth, as a radio operator gunner.

I became a sergeant, but always regretted not having become an officer. My best friend on our B-24 bomber crew was Joe, our navigator. Enlisted men and officers were not supposed to fraternize, but we sometimes did.

One day we went on leave together in Savannah. I asked Joe if he would exchange uniforms with me for a few hours so that I could feel like an officer. We went into the restroom of a nearby hotel and swapped uniforms. I then paraded the street as an officer, snappily returning salutes of the enlisted men who passed by.

Then "when the clock struck midnight," the charade ended, and I was back on the street saluting the silver bars that passed in the night. I could have wound up in the brig for impersonating an officer.

I'm a little embarrassed to reveal my next two forays into crime, because they were of a sexual nature, i.e., masturbation and consorting with a prostitute. I know that both are illegal in some places, but if you understand what a sordid life I led as a youth, you'll understand how easy it was for me to start stealing lunches at age eighty-four.

As a pimply thirteen-year-old I often found solace in reading lurid passages in *Balzac's Tales* in the bathroom. Too bad we didn't have *Playboy* in those days, but you have to play the cards you are dealt. That's all I'll have to say about the first of my sexual crimes. By the way, what's the statute of limitations for masturbation?

Eight years later I was twenty-one years old and in college in New Haven. (My two-year-plus Army Air Force stint came during my sophomore year in college.) One evening I went to a dime-a-dance ballroom in New York City in search of a "dance" lesson. ("So You Think You Can Dance" had a different meaning in those days.) I had heard from some college friends that the dance hostesses practiced a less honorable (but more profitable) profession after hours. I bought some dance tickets (yes, they cost more than ten cents apiece) and asked one of the hostesses to dance (let's call her Kim). She took all my tickets and seemed to take an instant liking to me (which is more than I can say for most of the girls that I dated from Smith, Sarah Lawrence, and Connecticut College For Women). Kim could soon feel that I liked her, as she tried to push her pelvic area through to my spine.

I propositioned her, and we agreed upon a price. The only trouble was Kim demanded payment up front. I reluctantly agreed and slipped her the cash. She squeezed my hand and favored me with a big wide smile and a wink that hinted at the sexual pleasures that lay ahead. My first impression was correct—she did like me.

Kim whispered in my ear that I should meet her after the place closed, which was at 3:00 a.m. She said she couldn't meet me right outside the dance hall because the boss didn't allow the girls to "date" the customers. I respected her discretion in this matter.

I can't remember what I did to while away the hours, but at three o'clock I stood erect a few blocks away at 47th Street and Broadway. Thirty minutes later I happened to glance across the street and noticed a man whom I had seen dancing with Kim. I went up to him and asked if he was waiting to meet her. He told me he had also paid for an after-hours date. We smiled sheepishly at each other, shook hands, and walked off into the night alone, with our tails between our legs. What a way to get stiffed by a prostitute.

I think that's why, to this very day, I don't like to dance.

My next foray into criminal activity happened in the 1960s. Marijuana smoking was on the rise, and even though Judy and I were heavy cigarette smokers, we never indulged in pot smoking until one day when a co-worker on Wall Street gave me a joint. I put it in the closet, too afraid to get involved. But come that New Year's Eve, we had nothing better to do, so we inhaled. We both had a bad trip because the pot was so old—it was a terrifying experience. I still remember my anguish when a thought popped into my head, disappeared, and then my mind went looking for it.

We smoked once or twice thereafter and finally got the hang of it. It wasn't easy to buy one cigarette every couple of months, so I hit upon an easy and cost-effective solution. We lived in an apartment on a high floor with a large terrace. I was quite a gardener in those days. (My garden appeared in the New York Times twice, showing off my vegetables and roses.)

I decided to increase the varieties under cultivation by adding marijuana (only for personal use, not as a cash crop). The plants flourished, and in a short while grew nine feet high.

Then one day, as I was standing in the lobby of our building, the woman who lived upstairs told me in a loud voice that her teenage daughter had spotted the plants growing upwards toward her window and that she planned to harvest some for her own use. I was scared s_ _ tless.

That night, under the cover of darkness, Jack cut down the beanstalk, and we rarely smoked again.

Well, there you have it. That's a recap of my "rap sheet," and I know you understand why I pursued a life of crime as an adult.

MY HERO IS A TUNA

I didn't enjoy my free lunch at The Gardens Cemetery today. It wasn't the quality of the half a tuna hero I ate. It was the eerie feeling walking around the halls of this two-story mausoleum and passing by the crypts of men with whom I had played tennis or been out to dinner. I bet they would only be too happy to change places with me, so I won't complain about the cuisine.

Here's a play-by-play of my hour-plus lunch and seminar at "…a cemetery like no other cemetery you have ever visited."

12:00 p.m. Check in. Led to elevator. Enter small meeting room. Only three couples in attendance. Very bad sign. Either the cemetery or the food must be lousy.

Room has four tables, sixteen chairs, four roast beef heroes, four tuna heroes, thirty-two Ritz crackers, one coffee urn (pun intended), plus accoutrements.

"Help yourself to lunch," greeter says. Others are not eating, so take a cup of coffee and try to appear nonchalant. It's not too difficult, because spread is not much more appealing than the one I had at cemetery in Ft. Lauderdale—and well below the attractiveness of the bagels and Nova Scotia salmon at the last funeral home. Next week have an appointment for a free lunch seminar given by another local

funeral home. It's going to be at a Chinese restaurant. Sounds like a joke, but it isn't. It's on Sunday night. I'll keep you posted.

Walk up to the counter and take half of both a tuna hero and roast beef hero. A tad better than hospital food. Sorry came out in this heat.

12:15 p.m. Speaker welcomes us. Not dressed like a schlump, even though he has the same physique as yesterday's speaker. Tie, long-sleeved shirt, and pressed slacks. No wife would complain.

Not surprised he's dressed so nattily because he starts off by saying his idol is Sy Syms. Why? Because Sy Syms believes that "an educated consumer is their best customer." Speaker wants us to be truly educated about the cemetery business—and if we are, he says we're sure to pick The Gardens as our final resting place.

Passes out quiz. Includes multiple-choice questions about the cemetery business and The Gardens. One woman gets into the spirit of things and enjoys spouting out the answers. Speaker calls her his best student. She's pleased. Bet she buys a crypt. Probably one of the most expensive on the second level.

Shirt and tie explains this cemetery only has crypts, no in-ground burials. Will have 150,000 bodies interred when fully completed and sold out—not chopped liver. Maybe heard him wrong. Maybe 15,000. I need a hearing aid.

Several cemetery office employees come in during talk and take a hero. Wonder if they are forced to come in and take a sandwich so it looks to the attendees that the food is edible.

Four Family Service Counselors (FSC) are waiting outside our room for their one-on-one meetings, like vultures circling above their prey. Know that's an exaggeration but like the ring of it. Have a mental flashback to our vacation trip to Tanzania when we were out on safari and were served a picnic lunch. All of a sudden a group of large birds swooped down and grabbed the sandwiches out of our hands. It was a very frightening experience. If the Tanzanian tour operator had served the same sandwiches that The Gardens Cemetery served, the birds would have stayed aloft.

"Any questions?" speaker asks. Felt like asking if we were free to take as many Ritz crackers as we wanted, but decided it might get back to Judy.

12:45 p.m. Dreaded one-on-one begins. "Any questions?" FSC asks. Inquire about the cost of the different crypts. "Best" is the couch type, which means both husband's and wife's caskets are in the same crypt without a wall in between. FSC pushes couch type ($30,000)—tells of husband who said he spent his whole life without a wall between himself and wife, so why would he want a wall between them in death. Guess his wife doesn't snore. Wonder if it's worth ten grand extra to be without a wall. Wonder if corpses snuggle. "Baby, it's cold inside."

Ask her about new Veteran's National Cemetery nearby where the funeral is free. She's not happy with the question, but she's prepared. "Caskets are in the ground, and the water table is very high in Florida, and eventually water surrounds the caskets and seeps in." I visualize my casket rolling around in water—I'd probably get seasick. She continues, "VA only gives you thirty minutes for funeral service—not a minute more—and they only have a small canopy that covers no more than fifteen people," she admonishes. Reply in jest that it would be good for someone who only has a small group of friends. She forces a tight smile. I decide to end discussion of this subject.

She says two caskets are included in the price of the special they are running till end of September. That's a five grand saving. Extras include opening and closing costs. And crypts can be electrified, she declares. Without thinking I ask why anyone would want a light inside his crypt. She chides me that the light goes on the outside of the marble wall. Want to ask if I can have a neon sign with a moveable message. Fantasize that I could be the first on my block (wall) to have one. One look at her face dissuades me from pursuing this line of inquiry.

She tells me she has sold crypts to 102 people who live in the same community as we do. That's fifty-one families out of six hundred or so. I'm impressed. She mentions names. Can you imagine name-dropping in a cemetery? She means well and just trying to make a living. (So am I; I like her chances better.)

1:15 p.m. FSC takes me on a tour to get the flavor of the place, but lose my appetite. Hallways lined with crypts six tiers high—some with lights burning twenty-four hours a day, some with receptacles for flowers. Here's where I come face to face with crypts of men I knew. Didn't know them well enough to have come to their funerals, but well enough to have their faces pop up in my mind. They are all encrypted on the most expensive second level. Reminds me of the expression, "It's good to have friends in the right places."

I'd be mortified to have to spend eternity on the top (cheapest) row. Can imagine one of my grandchildren coming to visit and pointing to the top tier and saying, "There's Grandpa way up there. Wonder why he wanted to be buried so far off the ground. Especially since he was acrophobic." That would be enough to make me turn over.

FSC tries to lighten things up, since she sees that the sight of vaults of some people I knew affects me. Tells story that one of the men joked that he wanted to use the electricity to put an ATM machine on the wall of his crypt so his children would come to visit him.

1:15 p.m. Decide good note to leave on. Thank FSC and can't wait to get out of there.

I furtively snapped a photo of the luncheon banquet. I don't know what I would have said to anyone who asked me why I was taking a picture of a plate of hero sandwiches in a mausoleum. The box of Ritz crackers was too shy to be photographed. The roll of Charmin was a nice touch. I was overwhelmed.

Who says there are no hero's at a mausoleum?

HOW TO RATE SEMINARS

**** Dinner is served

*** Lunch is served

** Breakfast is served

* Continental breakfast is served

¾* Coffee and dessert are served

½* Refreshments are served

¼* A sweet treat for all

A "+" is added for each of the following accoutrements:

Dessert

Beverage

Cloth tablecloth and napkin

Metal silverware

Free parking nearby

A "−" is assigned for each of the following negatives:

Meal is served at place of business. Meal is served at a cheap Chinese restaurant.

Meal is a sandwich.

Lecture lasts over 1½ hours.

Meal is served more than two hours before or after normal time for such a meal, i.e., dinner at 4:00 p.m. or breakfast at 10:00 a.m.

HOIST ON MY OWN PETARD

I met my match today, and all I had to show for my efforts was a lousy cup of tea in a drab Chinese restaurant. A smallish, drab man forenamed Ray shattered my vision of steamed dumplings and barbequed spare ribs, followed by a generous portion of roast duck. *Bye, bye, free lunch pie.*

Let me explain. At 11:15 a.m. I pulled my car into the parking lot of a strip mall next to Kings Point, one of the oldest communities in the area. I parked outside of Peking Palace, the Chinese restaurant that was to be the home of my free lunch seminar. It was to be hosted by a nearby memorial chapel. I was early, so I sat in the car to see how many people went into the restaurant. No one went in. You don't have to be the "Oracle at Kings Point" (a *yenta* in Yiddish, a busybody in English) to know that trouble lay ahead.

I cautiously ventured inside and viewed an empty, dreary dining room. "I'm here for the seminar, and I must be early," I said to the young hostess. She pointed in Chinese to a short man sitting in a small booth in the corner.

11:30 a.m. "You're Earl Bronsteen," the outstretched hand says. "I'm Ray." Couldn't for the life of me guess how he knew my name. "No one else seems to have shown up," he says as he ushers me to a seat

opposite him in the booth that soon began to feel like one of those interrogation rooms you see on crime shows on TV. (Where was Jack Bauer, now that I need him?)

Uneasily ask how many others were coming. He replies, "Eight were supposed to show up, but it looks like you're the only one. You'll still get your lunch after I explain our program." Furtively glance at the sheet in front of him and see that my name was the only one listed. Guess all's fair in the free lunch seminar business. I'm the last one to complain about not playing by the Marquess of Queensberry's Rules in a Chinese restaurant in a Jewish neighborhood.

Waiter pours some tea in my cup, and Ray starts on his pitch. Five thousand dollars for two burials, caskets (pine), and one funeral limo (black). Thousand-dollar discount for coming to the seminar. (Wanted to ask if I could have the thousand-dollar discount for all the people who didn't show up, but guessed Ray would say no.) Burial at Veteran's Cemetery is free. Forty-eight months to pay, no interest

"Do you have any questions?" he inquires. Ask one or two to be polite. "If you had brought your wife, she would have had some questions to ask," he admonishes. He was clearly disappointed in me. I felt I never lived up to Ray's expectations. Perhaps never will. Smile wanly.

"I'll write the contract up, and you have thirty days to cancel," Ray says as he takes out pen and contract form.

Look around to see if waiter was bringing my lunch, but room is deserted. Guess have to stall until chef gets the duck nice and crispy.

Tell him that I want to look at the VA Cemetery before I make a final decision. "You should have done that before you came here," he reprimands me. I had heard that the VA Cemetery had a ceremonial hall that would hold only fifteen people, and ask him about this deficiency. "No! There's room for thirty to forty people. You wouldn't have more mourners than that, would you?" Ray spit out the words in derision.

"What about my lunch?" I parry, with all the skill of a Jewish D'Artagnan.

"Go visit the VA Cemetery with your wife, come back next month to the seminar, and I'll treat you and your wife to lunch. How's that for a good deal?" Ray ripostes. He's as cool as Jack Nicholson in the movie Batman and come to think of it, he looks more than a little like the Joker.

"Are you going to pay for my tea?" I beseech. "Oh, all right," he answers.

On the way out of the still-empty restaurant, I asked the hostess for a menu. It listed forty different complete lunches, including soup, egg roll, fried rice (or brown), and tea, with prices ranging from $5.49 to $5.99. So, when all is said and done, Ray saved a fiver, and I saved a case of potential ptomaine poisoning at Peking Palace.

As I looked back into the restaurant, I thought I saw the hostess walk over to Ray and raise his right arm in victory, but that might just have been a figment of my imagination. I went next door and bought a pumpernickel bagel to take home to make a sandwich for my lunch.

I gave Ray's card to Judy and told her to put it in my Death file, so that she'll remember to invite him to my funeral. Then he can see how many mourners attend. I'll have the last laugh.

Educational PS. Have you ever wondered what the "petard" was that everyone's being hoisted by? Well, petard refers to an explosive device that was used to blast a breach in a wall. It comes from the French petard = a loud discharge of intestinal gas. "Hoist" refers to a crane that was used to put the bomb on or by the wall. So next time you use the expression, "Hoist by your own petard" in mixed company, you better make sure you haven't had beans for dinner.

INTERMEZZO #3

In the course of my research for this project, I've visited four funeral homes and/or cemeteries. You may not have noticed, but on most of these occasions it was raining—and every time I was reminded of my mother's funeral more than three decades ago.

During my second career as an installation artist, I created a multi-tiered array of cardboard boxes, each of which portrayed an incident in my life. Each box was cut out in the front, and inside I created a vignette depicting that event. A narrative was pasted to the outside. For mother's funeral box I placed a black umbrella and a pair of muddied black shoes, along with the following narrative:

It was a perfect day for a funeral. The rain poured down on the small group of mourners as we stood in the mud around the gravesite. We listened to the young rabbi speak of my ninety-two-year-old mother, who he had never met, and who he would never think of again. The family members' tear-stained eulogies summed up a good woman's long life in a few fleeting minutes.

The few mourners huddled under their umbrellas at the gravesite and thought about my mother's wonderful traits, her cruel and tortured last years (widowed early on and afflicted with Alzheimer's and blindness), their own departed loved ones, and their own mortality. I said my goodbyes with my umbrella pulled down over my face, embarrassed to show my tears. I wish I had said these words to her when she was alive.

The casket's highly polished exterior shed the raindrops as it lay perched above the deep hole that waited to claim its prize. The mumbled condolences of the leave takers brought the ceremony to an end. It was, indeed, a perfect day for a funeral.

I wonder if it will rain at my funeral. At least I won't get wet.

WHAT WILL TOMORROW BRING?

In less than twenty-four hours I would be registering for an investment seminar/luncheon at nearby LOLA Restaurant, and I was filled with trepidation. This event presented two new problems. First, the luncheon was being sponsored by a financial services company run by a man who lives in the same community as I do. Let's call him Harold. I have never met the man, but knew I would recognize him and probably vice versa. And I'll almost certainly keep running into him. Whenever he saw me, he would remember I'm the guy who ate his food, but didn't sign up as a client. I wondered if I should dye my hair and wear sunglasses.

The second problem is that the invitation I received in the mail had an asterisk after the words "Complimentary lunch." The small print specified that the free lunch was for "prospective clients only." This was a new wrinkle, and I wondered how my host was going to decide who was a prospective client.

I could picture myself hooked up to a lie detector machine in the marbled men's room. "Are you now, or have you been, a freeloader?" the man sitting by the machine with its rapidly fluctuating needle asks. As I considered what response I should make to the question that will decide whether I can enjoy LOLA Restaurant's Chef Bruno Silva's plat du jour, I visualized the men's room attendant advising me to answer yes. I imagined he knows what they do to people who lie to the financial planner's inquisitor.

I understand there is some sort of drug that you can take to beat a lie detector. I remember seeing it work on one of those spy series on TV recently. I wondered how much the drug costs and if there are any serious side effects. Well, I'll just have to take my chances. It's all part of the job.

PS. LOLA stands for Love Often, Laugh Alot. We'll see who's laughing a lot at noon tomorrow. A while ago we received a $20 gift card from LOLA's and never used it. If the food is good tomorrow, maybe I'll put the gift card to use next week and take advantage of their advertised special of "2 appetizers, 2 entrees, 2 desserts for $22 person." If I could get Herb to go along and pay his share, I'd only have to kick in two bucks for dinner. Sounds good to me.

TOMORROW IS TODAY

I pulled my car into a nearly empty parking lot at LOLA Restaurant at 10:40 a.m., glanced at the menu in the window, and walked into a nearly empty, large, open dining room and bar. It featured very modern décor, especially the very pregnant hostess. She was certainly a far cry from the shapely hostesses you find in most of this area's tonier eating establishments. Must be the restaurant owner's wife, or worse. I'm guided toward two pinstriped gray suits. We shook hands. I smiled. They checked off my name. They say Harold (my neighbor and the chief honcho of the sponsor) is not coming. I gave a big sigh of relief. I went to the men's room and took off my sunglasses and dark-haired wig.

10:55 a.m. Directed to a chair in the middle of a U-shaped table arrangement, with seventeen place settings facing a projector and screen. Knife, fork, cloth napkin, water glass, and bread and butter plate. No spoon. Figure iced tea is fifty/fifty at best.

Four empty chairs at the table. Suit places call and announces more people are on the way and promises program will start in a few minutes. Wonder if the four absentees do not show up for lunch, whether they'll let me have seconds.

Woman arrives. Tells suit that the address given on the invitation to the restaurant is wrong and that's why she's late. No problem, he assures her. She is directed to chair next to me. Asks me if Harold is here. She's disappointed when I tell her no. She tells me she wanted to meet him because she has heard good things about him.

10:45 a.m. Miguel asks what I'd like to drink. "Iced tea," I reply, as do most of the guests. Look around. Don't recognize anyone from my community or from any previous free lunch seminar I've attended. Mostly grey hair; mostly women, some with the aura of a freeloader. Wonder if my aura is showing.

10:50 Iced tea arrives. Passion fruit-flavored tea. (Piss-elegant tea.)

11:02 a.m. Bread arrives with olive oil and spices dip. Warm, very tasty. Only have one piece because I started on a diet yesterday.

Miguel asks, "Turkey wrap or Chicken Milanese?" Choose the latter.

11:05 a.m. Two more people show up, and Marvin, one of the suits, takes microphone and turns on projector. Tells us about his company. Sounds impressive. Over five hundred employees and offices in four states. They offer bonds, mutual funds, and REITS.

11:10 a.m. Finish iced tea. Wonder if there will be refills. Sixty/forty, I guess.

11:20 a.m. Gordy, the other suit, takes mike to pitch their ninth in-house REIT. He pronounces it "Writ." They have a $2 billion offering in progress, of which 80 percent has been sold. He describes it as "The best thing since sliced bread." Makes me hungry; decide to go off my diet and have a second piece of bread. Dip into dip. Yummy.

Iced tea refill arrives. Good and bad. The sugar bowl is still out of reach, and it would be impolite to ask my neighbor for a packet while Gordy is talking. He explains how their REITs work. They buy Hampton Inn and Hilton Extended-Stay Hotels for cash. Pays investors 7 percent, sounds good. Maybe too good, maybe not good enough. Hard to swallow, but guests are eating it up.

Neighbor on left asks me to pass the empty bread and butter plate on my right. I ask him to slip a Splenda. Good trade.

11:30 a.m. Have been scribbling away furiously so that I can bring you a blow-by-blow account. Notice a lady at the other end of the table making a lot of notes. I'm fearful. Could there be someone else out there who is writing a book about free lunch seminars? She seems pretty old, but then again, so am I. She'll bear watching.

One half hour to go till lunch is served. Can smell the chicken being Milanesed.

11:45 p.m. Four customers enter the otherwise-empty restaurant for lunch and are seated in the far corner. Recognize one of them and slink into my chair. I'd be embarrassed to be seen needing a free meal. He doesn't glance my way. My wig and dark glasses are at the ready.

They are all evidently slightly hard of hearing, and their conversation partially drowns out our speaker.

Woman who was taking notes has a glazed look on her face from the overly detailed description of their REITs. No pen to be seen. I'm in the clear.

12:00 a.m. Gordy finishes pitch for their REIT, and the other suit sums up. Says all their investments are registered with the SEC. Woman asks what does registered with SEC mean. "Are they guaranteed?" she asks. "No," he replies, "but Madoffs weren't registered. That's why his investors lost all their money."

Suit says the reason their REIT can pay 7 percent is that a REIT doesn't have to pay corporate taxes. No one questions his conclusion.

Woman asks what is the commission charge. "Nothing," suit says. As he tries to explain why, it seems that his nose gets larger and larger. Finally he relates that his company gets a 10 percent commission. He tries to convey the impression that the investor doesn't pay any commission, because the money comes out of the REIT. Can't tell if he *convinced anyone. If Harold's company sells out this offering, he'll rake in a cool $200 million, less the $500 or so he has to pay for our lunch. This is his ninth offering. He's rolling in dough. Sure he'll have dessert for us. It would be as easy as pie.*

Someone asks what is the minimum investment. Speaker says a program like theirs is usually available only to hedge funds, but we can get in for as little as five grand.

Says lunch is on its way. Everyone applauds. Pick up my fork. Neighbor looks at me. Put fork down halfway.

12:08 p.m. Miguel places plate in front of me. Drizzled greens on top. Chicken hidden underneath to disguise the quantity. Tasty, but not hot. Maybe not supposed to be hot. My neighbor's turkey wrap looks fine, and it's garnished with chips. I made the right choice— mine must cost more.

Suit praises the food. "That's a good-looking lunch!" We all agree. No dessert, but this is partially offset by the fact that there is no pressure to set up a one-on-one appointment. "Call us if you want some more information." was the only sales pitch. Pretty classy.

12:22 p.m. One of the ladies asks for a doggie bag for the rest of her turkey wrap. Show me a doggie bag taker-outer at a free lunch seminar, and I'll show you a freeloader.

I bid my adieus and asked the fecund hostess for a menu on the way out of the almost-deserted restaurant. Once I was back in my car, I scanned the menu. My Chicken Milanese listed for $21. All in all, I got my money's worth.

I only hope that Harold doesn't check the names and addresses of the attendees. I'm not going to answer the doorbell for the next month.

Eat by numbers.

1. Earl Bronsteen
2. Neighbor who asked me (See #1) to pass a butter plate (see #3)
3. His butter plate
4. My butter plate with two Splenda packets for my iced tea (see #8)
5. Warm bread
6. Cloth napkin
7. Dip for bread
8. Iced tea with lemon wedge

PS. I received the inevitable follow-up call from one of the pleasant, polite, pinstriped suits asking if I wanted any more information about bonds or their REIT. In response to my noncommittal reply, he told me that they sold $90 million of the new REIT in August and $84 million in July. I parried by answering that they must have given a helluva lot of luncheons in the past two months. He laughed and reported that they have these seminars going in all four states.

He reminded me that they have had eight previous REITS, and no one has lost a penny. The lowest return was 5 percent, and the highest, 15 percent. When I replied, "I'm not sure if I have the money right now," he tried to checkmate me by adding that the minimum investment was $5,000.

I was in a quandary. If I said," I don't have five thousand dollars to invest," I'd sure look like a loser who was only at the seminar for a free lunch. I thanked him for his help and told him I'd let him know if I changed my mind. I appreciated his soft-sell approach, the Chicken Milanese, and the lack of pressure, but not enough to invest in his real estate deal right now. I wondered what they call Chicken Milanese in Milan, probably Chicken New York.

All I can think of is that since the company raked in a cool $17 million in commissions (10 percent of $174 million) in the past two months, they should have stepped up to the plate and served us dessert (baked Alaska, at the very least).

LOBSTER VS. DANISH

A Boca Raton insurance agency ran a full-page ad last Sunday in the local paper touting a:

FREE ANNUITY SEMINAR

7–9 p.m.

Boca Raton Marriot

My salivary juices started to flow at the prospect of another free meal at an expensive restaurant. I happen to know that this ad costs just north of $10,000. Perhaps this will be my first free meal at which lobster is served. I prefer broiled to steamed.

Imagine my astonishment when I read the small print:

Join us for coffee and dessert.

Can you imagine anyone going out after dinner to be subjected to a two-hour speech on the boring subject of annuities, just for a cup of coffee and dessert? I don't drink coffee, and I'm on a diet.

To make matters worse, I happen to know the man who owns this insurance agency. He lives in a $15 million home and could afford to serve five-pound lobsters to everyone who attends this seminar.

To make matters worse, things are so slow in the free lunch seminar business in late August that I'm going to go to the seminar. I'll lose my professional standing if anyone sees me there—with a cup of coffee in one hand and nosh of Danish in the other—but unless I keep my hand in, I'll lose my touch. If I have to pay for valet parking, the whole evening will be a wash.

To make matters worse, the full-page ad ran again today (at a cost of more than $4,000 for a weekday edition), and it still only offers coffee and dessert as a come-on. Don't they realize that if he had offered lobster instead of coffee and dessert in their first ad, they would not have had to run a second?

Fast forward to 7:00 p.m. Monday, August 30, 2010. The parking lot at the Boca Marriot was extremely crowded. I wondered if the crowd was there for the seminar or just people coming for or having affairs. The fancy lobby featured a pitcher of water filled with cucumbers, courtesy of Marriot, but I decided not to indulge. Maybe I'll bring my tennis partners here after our next game.

I walked through the lobby and was met by a genial man who pointed the way to the seminar and joked, "This way to the bar mitzvah. Leave your gifts on the table on the left." Everyone smiled politely. I signed in and got a handful of booklets.

The large ballroom was filled with seventeen rows of tables each with twelve chairs. Wow! Two hundred people coming for dessert and coffee. Sure sign that the economic recovery has a long way to go. I'd better call Barack, or we'll likely see Sarah in the Oval Office in 2012. (If you're a Republican, please just switch the names around.)

7:05 p.m. Feeding frenzy at the refreshment table—various cakes, fresh fruit, coffees, and soft drinks. As I take a picture, get a strange look from those in line who are here to do some serious eating.

Push my way through and only take some fruit and a cup of coffee. Thumb my nose at the calorie-laden cheesecake and chocolate mousse slices.

Feel as virtuous as Malvolio as I leave the "cakes and ale" to the others. Take a seat in the last row on the far end (just like in college). No one will see me here.

Survey crowd. Younger than typical Boca residents. Every seat taken. Ten guests standing. After finish eating my fruit and coffee, consider leaving and figure no one would be the wiser. Just received a new DVD at home from Netflix featuring a detective mystery from Masterpiece Theater; pretty sure it would be more entertaining than a speech about annuities. But Howard is sitting in a chair by the door. Afraid he might recognize me. His father bought my previous house to tear down and make into a sculpture garden as an annex to his mansion. Decide to stay and tough it out for the next two hours. Many people going back for seconds on dessert. Thirds? Who's counting? Howard?

7:10 p.m. Speaker welcomes huge crowd. Says this is XYZ's Insurance Agency's first-ever seminar on annuities and first ever in the evening. Size of the crowd indicates they made a smart move. Introduces Howard. He has the figure, presence, and stentorian voice of a young Pavarotti. Great speaker.

Howard introduces his director of annuity marketing, Lee, who turns out to be same man who made the joke about bar mitzvahs as I entered. He's no Pavarotti, no JFK, but sure seems to know his Bermudas—but how does a layman, no matter how intelligent, know if what he's being told is true and complete? For example, he mentions that one of the firm's competitors runs seminars at Morton's and that he instructs everyone to convert their Keogh Plans to Roth IRAs. (I remember; I was there. It was the lunch of the schlump.) Lee contradicts him. Alleges only in the rarest of cases does it pay for someone to do so. (Query: Do you believe a speaker who serves up a free steak dinner or one who provides only dessert and coffee?)

In connection with some point, which I can't remember, Lee asks, "Are there any doctors in the room?" Not one of the 167 people raises his hand. Lee quickly recovers and asks, "Has anyone ever been to a doctor?" Laughs all around.

8:30 p.m. He finishes. Asks, "Have you heard more and learned more about annuities this evening than ever before?" Crowd roars its approval. I agree. It's the best presentation anyone has made at any of the seminars I've been to so far. It's even possible that Judy and I might be interested. Maybe I'll suggest to Lee that we discuss it over lunch.

Lee asks, "Any questions?" Ask a question about Judy's long-term heath-care policy in relation to a point he made. "Great question," he replies and then gives an answer. Raise my hand again. "Great answer, but that wasn't to the question I asked," I reply. Laughs. Repeat question and get an answer.

Howard takes over the mike. Asks audience, "How many people now own an annuity?" Three quarters raise their hands.

"How many people are looking to buy an annuity?" he inquires. Maybe two hands are raised. I'm very surprised. Guests must fear they'd be carted away to the next room and have to sign up on the spot. Howard gets the same minimal response when he asks, "How many people are looking to buy life insurance?" And only six hands are raised in reply to the same question about buying long-term health care. This crowd is a tough sell.

Our host must be sorry he let people have seconds.

Howard tells story how his father (Barry) lost all of his (Howard's) bar mitzvah money by buying Gulf & Western Stock for him.

His mother (Carole) made his dad replenish the kitty. They are seen dancing at some charity function.

You can be insured they're having a good time.

Since then Howard says he's been afraid of the stock market. He's sure everyone in the audience is queasy about leaving their money in the stock market. Then he summarizes evening's theme: Annuities are the way to get a better yield for your funds than leaving it in bank accounts and CDs. And there is no risk (no insurance carrier has ever reneged on principal or interest), and some upside potential if the market rises. Thanks us all for coming.

8:50 p.m. Howard calls it quits. Great applause. Only a few people leave before the end.

I drove home and was too tired to type up my notes of the evening's events. I kissed Judy good night and dropped into bed, where I tossed and turned. Maybe the coffee was not decaf.

I dreamed of Pavarotti force-feeding cheesecake down Malvolio's throat while Barry sang "O Sole Mio" to Carole as they danced off into the sunset.

SEPTEMBER COMES IN LIKE A LAMB

I drew a complete blank in my quest for seminars during the first two weeks of September.

The Cleveland Clinic offered a "light lunch," but I didn't want to drive forty-five minutes to hear a talk on rotator cuff pain. I don't like to go into hospitals unless I have to. I don't know which is more dangerous, going into a hospital's operating room for heart surgery or going into a hospital's dining room for a light lunch.

I spent two weeks moping around the house. But my spirits were lifted by a flurry of newspaper announcements and mailings that resulted in five appointments for the rest of September. This activity would help take my mind off my scheduled CAT scan appointment on September 27, which will determine how fast my lymphoma is growing and when my next round of chemo will start. But not to worry, I've had lymphoma for twenty years, and it hasn't interfered with my freeloading one bit.

I don't want to spoil your enjoyment of reading my chronicling of tomorrow's adventures (Tuesday, September 14) by giving away the ending—but I have another doubleheader scheduled for that day, with a haircut sandwiched in between.

I hope I can get to sleep tonight. Judy is away in California, so I can wear whatever I damn well please tomorrow.

SEPTEMBER'S SLUMP SAVED BY SCHLUMP

Let's backtrack to Monday morning, September 13. As I read the local newspaper over the breakfast table, a full-page ad seemed to mock me. It was from the same financial services company that had served up (at their seminar last month on IRAs at Morton's) a sizzling filet mignon that was too rare—and which I was too chicken to send back. You might not remember that I recounted how the woman sitting next to me had denigrated the speaker's attire by referring to him as a schlump. Well, regardless of his lack of sartorial splendor, it seemed as if my host at that previous dinner was trying to make amends for the underdone steak by offering me another free meal. I'm not one to look a gift horse in the mouth, but this seminar was to be at Carrabba's, quite a step down from Morton's, and they sure weren't going to serve filet mignon—more likely pasta or pizza. But what the hell. I've seen a lot of TV commercials for the restaurant, and Johnny Carrraba and his partner sure look the part of great Italian chefs. I wouldn't mind a change of pace in my fare anyway.

The subject matter of the second seminar was annuities, which is different from that of the first. I phoned to make a reservation, but just in case they don't permit people who attended the other seminar to attend this one, I took the precaution of leaving my cell phone number. (I think I got the idea from watching Jack Bauer on 24.)

The telephone receptionist had a stern tone and warned me to be sure to bring my appointment calendar to the seminar (meaning that at the seminar I couldn't use the lame excuse of not having my calendar with me as the reason for not being able to make a follow-up appointment on the spot). I sure wouldn't like to be the one who forgets to bring his calendar appointment book and has to face her wrath. She also wanted me to assure her that I'd be around the next two weeks. She alerted me that she'd be calling Tuesday to confirm Wednesday's seminar. I could hardly wait to see what else I'd have to promise her. Dominatrix, to be sure.

I didn't sleep too well that night with all the excitement of the doubleheader coming up the next day.

DUMPED BY THE SCHLUMP

After eating a light breakfast, I pulled away in my 2006 Toyota Matrix for the trip to Red Lobster for today's first seminar. Just as I hit the road, my cell phone rang. It was from the financial services company—but who is on the phone—not the cruel and pitiless telephone receptionist I had spoken to before, but the head of the company. He called to apologize because he had to cancel the seminar and said he would make it up to me by sending info on subsequent seminars. We chatted amiably on the phone for a few minutes. He asked if I had any annuities. I said no. More small talk. "How old are you?" he interrogated.

"Eighty," I lied.

"How old is your wife?"

"Seventy," I responded. (I can't tell you if this was a lie or not.)

"You robbed the cradle," he joshed. Call ends.

As I drove north toward Lake Worth, the heavens opened up, and I hydroplaned through a torrential downpour for half an hour. You may remember the same thing happened on my way to the cemetery in Ft. Lauderdale; and here I was on my way to a seminar on cremation sponsored by a company that owned cemeteries as well as crematoriums. I wondered if someone up there was trying to tell me something.

But the skies lifted as I entered the empty Red Lobster parking lot at 10:50 a.m. The only spaces that were already taken were the "Handicapped Parking" spots. I watched as a man tried the front door, to no avail. I felt a momentary panic. Perhaps the seminar was cancelled. A few minutes later he tried again, and this time he was let in with his wife

A large sign over the front door heralded, "Lunches starting at $6.99." I took this as a personal challenge to pick out an item for lunch that cost more. Sort of my way of attempting to climb Mount Everest without a Sherpa.

The door was locked, but after knocking I was admitted by a young woman in shirt and slacks who I mistook for a hostess. It later turned out she was the key speaker at the seminar.

There was a lobster tank by the door, and I asked her if that's what we're having for lunch. "I wish it," she replied. In response to my next question, she pointed toward the men's room.

The bathroom was a far cry from the marble palaces at Morton's and Ruth's Chris, and no Muzak, but far better in one respect— the sign above the sink read, "Employees Must *Double Wash* Their Hands!" (Sign doesn't speak well of their staff.)

11:10 a.m. It's so cold in restaurant, go out to get my sweater. There's a couple walking toward the door and inform them that it's freezing inside. The woman points to sweater she is carrying and says, "Us old folks are always thinking!" It's obvious Red Lobster attracts an intellectual crowd.

Enter back room of restaurant. Take seat at far end at an empty table set for five. There are place settings for thirty-eight people in the

room, and they are half-filled with elderly, very casually dressed guests with seemingly modest incomes.

Three men in suits and one other woman in a dress are there representing the hosts. Notice one of the men from the crematorium has grey/white flakes on his jacket collar. Wonder if it is a bad case of dandruff or just the fallout from that morning's cremation (Chernobyl Lite).

Menu is on the table, along with paper napkin, plus knife and fork (no dessert again). Six entrée choices—five fish and one Caesar salad with chicken. Want to ask the waitress which is the most expensive, but decide to gamble and pick the chicken. Server comes to take my drink order. It's so cold in the room that I ask for hot tea. She's taken aback, but agrees. Overhear a man at another table order a Bloody Mary a la carte. I wonder if it's his first drink of the day.

Put on nametag. I'm the only one at my table. Sitting way back in left field. Suit sits down next to me, and I'm faced with a one-on-one again. Works for the cemetery that is affiliated with the seminar. Very gentlemanly, non-pushy, ex-chief of police at Midwestern college. Jimmy Stewart comes to Red Lobster. He's so nice, sorry I can't be buried at his cemetery. Maybe next time!

11:10 a.m. Hot tea arrives. So many people had complained about the frigid temperatures that the AC was turned off, and now it's too hot for the tea. Take off my sweater. Wonder if the lobsters in the tank are bothered by the changes in temperature. They were huddled in one corner and seemed to be trying to wrap their arms around their bodies to warm themselves, but they couldn't because of the constricting rubber bands on their claws.

11:20 a.m. Hostess/moderator addresses group of sixteen of us for about half an hour. Tells group that her company is largest crematorium outfit in the world. Wonder what their gas bill is each month. "What's the price of a cremation?" comes from a front table.

"It's $989 for a basic cremation," she responds. She is pressed for more details as to what is included and what is not in the basic cremation. It appears to me that a more appropriate name would be "Bare Bones Cremation." For example, matches are extra in the $989 basic cremation.

"If I sign up today, do I get a discount?" "Do I get discount if both wife and I sign up?" "Why not a buy one, get one free, deal?" "Do you know what your competitor's prices are?"

Guests are very cost conscious. They obviously don't have money to burn.

Speaker answers that their prices are very competitive, and they have high standards, and quality control is a priority; "Twenty-four-hour phone service answered by a live American," she proudly announces. Asian woman winces.

One item that particularly appealed to me was their "Boat Charter Program." If you want to have your ashes cast over the seas, you pay an additional $325, and a boat captain will take your ashes out to international waters and cast them overboard. And for an additional $75, four guests can accompany the boat and watch the ceremony. Wanted to throw caution to the winds and ask (just for the halibut) how much it would cost to rent four fishing rods to use on the way home.

A few days after I wrote these words, I came upon an article in our local paper that made me out to be a prophet of sorts.

FORT LAUDERDALE—A burial in his beloved sea was the wish of Daniel Lansing who died last week at his home in Hickory, N.C. His family chartered a local fishing boat, and along with the boat's captain and crew, motored four miles offshore from Port

Everglades. They tendered their final good-byes and consigned Danny to the deep. Family members then fished for a spell in his memory.

I'm afraid this story doesn't have a happy ending. No, it wasn't that the family members came up empty-handed in their fishing exploits. It was that poor Daniel's body resurfaced a day later and caused quite a stir when it was taken to police headquarters.

11:30 a.m. Woman asks, "How do I know I am getting my husband's ashes back from the crematorium and not someone else's?" Moderator tells about their nine-step ID program that is keyed around a metal ID tag placed on the deceased's body and which is not destroyed in the conflagration. Woman asks what kind of metal will withstand that temperature. No one answers. No one else seems to care.

11:35 a.m. Man from cemetery takes over. He looks typecast for the part. When he looks at you, his steely eyes are riveted on yours. Announces sharply reduced prices on having your urn placed in their cemetery. Sounds so good, makes me yearn to try on an urn for size.

Romantic interlude follows when the speaker reports that they have a plan for a married couple whereby the ashes of the first to die will be held and commingled with the ashes of the second to die. Can just visualize the wife saying, "I have a headache. I'd rather be alone."

Man asks if an autopsy is mandatory in Florida. He wife looks at him quizzically. He's the same guy who had the 11:00 a.m. Bloody Mary. If I were his wife, I'd sleep with one eye open from now on.

As a wrap-up, moderator asks everyone to fill out info sheet, which has questions about her lecture and also place to sign up for a future one-on-one meeting. Everyone who hands this in is eligible for drawing for a gift certificate at Red Lobster (bet it's for $6.99).

12:10 p.m. Caesar salad and chicken arrive, accompanied by a delicious butter-laden biscuit. Guest asks for more biscuits, and a fresh basket is brought to each table. I refrain.

12:20 p.m. One of the hosts notices that the elderly man and his wife at the next table have eaten only part of their lunch.

"How's the food?" he asks the man, whose wife had left for the ladies room.

Husband responds, "We just had lunch before we came, because we didn't realize that food was being served."

When his wife returns, the husband explains the conversation he had just had. His wife asks why he gave that response." Well, I had to say something," he replies.

They had the rest of their food wrapped to go—no doubt this would be their dinner.

A cheerless ending to the meal.

12:25 p.m. Drawing is held. Was sure they would rig it to make one of those who signed up for a follow-up meeting the winner, but no, it was on the up and up. I did not win.

Thought they might have souvenirs for the rest of us, like a key-chain for the men or a necklace for the women, each with a miniature charm in the form of an urn attached.

No such luck, so pocketed three ballpoint pens bearing the words "National Crematorium" from the empty place settings at my table and left. I'll use it when I send out condolence letters.

I drove south with time to kill before my haircut and 3:30 p.m. seminar in Boca.

Veteran's National Cemetery

I passed the new Veteran's National Cemetery and decided to take a look. Burial is almost free for a veteran and his wife, and I wanted to check it out. It's laid out beautifully, just like Arlington—a sobering sight. I'd be proud to be buried here. And the price is right.

I got back into my car and drove off to my haircutting salon. In and out in thirteen minutes. It cost a little less than $1 per minute, including a $2 tip. I felt and looked like a new man. At 3:30 p.m. I entered Poppy's Restaurant. You may have wondered why I've never mentioned what the second seminar is about or what is being served. Well, I'm a bit embarrassed to tell you that the only blandishments listed in the ad for the seminar were, "Refreshments." But don't judge me too harshly, because the topic for the meeting was spinal stenosis, and I have it.

The ad talked about "minimally invasive spine surgery," so I thought I'd go listen and also find out what the word "refreshments" means to a surgeon. I'm still not sure that I'd want anyone operating on my spinal column, but I may go to his office for a visit, because the doctor mentioned other non—surgical possibilities. Maybe he has a food bar in his waiting room.

The refreshments served at the seminar consisted of one bite-size pastry, one mini Danish, and all the coffee you could drink. I ate the Danish and looked around at the table to see if there was anything I could take home. But finding nothing of value, I headed back home and soon dropped into bed. I wondered if I'd dream of being burned alive in a crematorium or just have a nightmare about being crippled by a slip of the surgeon's knife on my spine. It took quite a while before I fell asleep.

I woke up with a start after having had a bad dream. I had died and surprisingly enough gone to Heaven. I say "surprisingly' because I don't believe in an afterlife. Be that as it may, the dream unfolded in a barbershop. I was seated in a chair in a white gown and Grace Kelly was manicuring my nails. She was wearing the nightgown from her role in "Rear Window". There was a sign above the door, "Cleanliness is next to G-dliness". It was signed "anonymous".

Then I was on my way in search of a lunch seminar (free naturally up there.) I got into my solar powered Segway and rode to a fancy steak restaurant — and up there fancy is really fancy. Ruth had arrived a few years before me and already owned steak palaces all over Heaven.

But how could there be any financial seminars in Heaven? Certainly no one from Bears Stearns, Citigroup, Lehman Brothers, Goldman Sachs, and for that matter any of the large Wall Street investment firms would be up there.

And there would have been no need for seminars selling annuities, retirement facilities, cemeteries or the like. The only seminar I could find was one offering to sell private séances to the attendees so they could contact one's family back on Earth. It was a sort of intergalactic Skype. P. T. Barnum was the fast talking pitchman. I woke up just after I had raised my hand to sign up.

GOOD NEWS AND BAD NEWS

"Would you like to order salmon or filet mignon for your lunch this Thursday?" the pleasant voice on the telephone asked when she called to confirm my appointment for a seminar at a life care retirement community in the Palm Beach area. I had been hesitant about going to their seminar, because it was fifty-one minutes away—gas would cost about $14 for the round trip—but the magic words (filet mignon) sealed the deal for me. That's the good news.

And then Tuesday afternoon the same congenial voice called to tell me that the seminar has been cancelled because of construction work being done on the grounds. I wished I had ordered salmon instead of filet mignon, so I wouldn't be so disappointed. The caller said she'd telephone to reschedule. Maybe she will, maybe she won't. It's no skin off my back.

The other bad news isn't all that bad, considering that the life of a free lunch junkie is not always a bed of roasts. Before this last-minute cancellation I had called to make a reservation for a seminar that was to be held at the local Marriot the same evening as the retirement community filet lunch. I love doubleheaders. They really get my juices flowing. When I called, I was told that the seminar was sold out. If I had been wearing a pacemaker, I'm sure it would have kicked in. But not to worry. The voice on the phone said that there was a makeup seminar the very next day.

The meeting was to be held at Toojay's Deli, and it was to be for lunch instead of dinner. Freeloaders can't be choosers, so I signed up. I didn't feel too badly because a group meal at The Marriot is a gamble at best and a pastrami sandwich at Toojay's is to die for (or to die from, depending on your cholesterol level.

10:00 a.m. Enter Toojay's and am surprised to find quite a few diners sitting at tables having a late breakfast. Walk to the back and find a section of booths that have been cordoned off. Small sign on stand indicates am in the right place. Take a seat behind group of five who are chatting away noisily. My tablemate (Helen) is a widowed seventyish, grey-haired, and grayish-faced thin woman who looks a little like an older version of the woman with the farmer in Grant Woods' American Gothic. Helen has had neck pain for quite awhile, and that's why she came to this seminar, "Relief for Your Back and Neck Pain."

10:05 a.m. Looks like fewer than twenty people in attendance. Surprised because a seminar went to a week or so ago on same subject had about fifty people, and the surgeon gave away only coffee and Danish—here we're getting a full brunch. Wonder the significance of this discrepancy. Don't have time to ponder this conundrum, because a woman announces the doctor will be late and tells us to help ourselves to the food.

We advance upon the table from both sides, forming two phalanxes with our spears raised. Table is laden with platters of Nova Scotia salmon, whitefish, cream cheese, bagels of all description, onions, tomatoes, Danish, and coffee. No pastrami, but this is even better and less cholesterol. Hard to believe just finished breakfast two hours earlier. Don't know which of the goodies to pile on my plate. But problem is solved when notice a price list that shows that the Nova is $13.75 a half pound, and the whitefish is only $6.50. Pile on the Nova and wonder if got my pound of fish.

Helen sits back down with a full plate. Tells me she and her husband only went to a few seminars when he was alive, but never bought anything. Asks me where I live. Give a vague answer, and she persists until I name the development I live in. She nods approvingly. Tells me her husband used to play golf there. We find we have something else in common, because we both were born in Brooklyn, where she lived till they moved to Florida.

1. Nova Scotia Salmon—$27.50 per lb. 2. Whitefish—$13.00 per lb. 3. More Nova with onions, tomatoes, capers and lemon. 4. Cream cheese—$5.99 per lb. 5. Danish—$1.75 each. 6. Bagels—75 cents each. 7. Belly Rolls—Priceless.

10:20 a.m. Surgeon appears. Apologizes for lateness. Lean, vegetarian, sixty-or-so. Thirty-five years in practice. Launches into PowerPoint presentation about "How to Avoid the KNIFE." He talks about all the things he and his staff can do with medicines, therapy, etc., for those with back and neck pain to avoid surgery, but I can tell he hopes we all need surgery. You don't cover the overhead of his four offices by prescribing a few pills.

His cell phone goes off, and the doctor takes the call and converses for quite awhile. Use this interruption to refill my plate. He doesn't answer when his phone rings again. Wonder if I would have gone for thirds if he had. Helen notices I'm taking a lot of notes. I give my usual response. She says, "I used to be a secretary."

Doctor rushes to finish, because we have to vacate our booths for Toojay's lunch crowd. Opens the floor to questions. Each person asks personal question about his own problem. Answer generally is, "See me." Someone asks about acupuncture. He replies, "I understand it works well in China." He likes inner-spring mattresses and yoga. Says he exercises every day. Looks it. One of the attendees queries a sales rep from Stryker Corporation (the multi-billion-dollar medical parts supplier who paid for our luncheon on behalf of the surgeon who uses their products) about FDA recalls of some of their hip replacement products. He lies in response, "Never heard of it."

What do I care? Lunch was great. Wasn't my hip that was being gored. Helen mentions that her late husband died of lung cancer. Reply that I have lymphoma. She offers to get me some chicken soup. Boca has the most compassionate widows.

11:00 a.m. Time is up. Bid Helen good-bye. On my way out have to pass our food table—the whitefish looks up at me imploringly and winks—but I'm steadfast. Know I'll be sorry in an hour. Wave good-bye to the hard salamis on the wall and rush home to my large-sized bottle of Tums.

PS. Several days later I received a phone call from a nurse at the surgeon's office. I was sure she was calling to have me come in for a consultation with the surgeon, but no, she asked me if it was OK for her to give my phone number to Helen (my widowed tablemate at the seminar). I ask her what's it all about. It seems Helen told her that I had given her my phone number during the seminar, but she had left the piece of paper on the table by mistake, and that she thought I was widowed. I told the nurse that if Judy found out what Helen was trying to pull, she (Helen) better be careful or she'd be joining her deceased husband sooner than she had planned.

I studied my reflection in the mirror before I went to sleep that night. Not so bad for an old man. First woman to make a play for me since the third grade.

INTERMEZZO #4

October belongs to Reggie Jackson, but my feats this month may outdo his baseball heroics in the World Series. I'll let you be the judge. In the ten days from October 5 to 14, about the length of time of Reggie's "Mr. October" feats, I have four free lunch seminars and four doctor's appointments scheduled. The physicians include oncologist, dermatologist, dentist, and last, but not least, a spine surgeon.

"Not the spine surgeon whose seminar you attended last month at Poppy's Restaurant?" you ask yourself aloud. Yes, it's the very same tightfisted doctor who dished out only a mini-Danish and coffee as the fare to the attendees. I've had spinal stenosis for many years, and my walking is labored. He proclaimed at the seminar that 95 percent of the people who came to him did not need surgery, and I'm only going to see him because I plan to be in the 5 percent. His talk about minimally invasive surgery doesn't strike a responsive cord with my spine.

I mention this to assuage those of my readers who think I only go to these seminars to grab a free meal and then to capitalize by writing a best seller about my adventures.

Let me add one curious coincidence. I've never had pain in my back. My problem is in my thighs and legs. It may be a pinched nerve in my spinal cord that caused the problems I have walking. You are not going to believe what I have to tell you next, but it's true. I started to have a pain in my lower back a few days after having gone to this surgeon's seminar. It was the last straw that made me decide to call the doctor for an appointment. Frankly, I think it is quite possible that the surgeon laced the Danish he served at the seminar with a drug that causes temporary symptoms of back pain. Call me paranoid, if you want. I'm only 95 percent sure; that's why I'm still going to keep the appointment.

The three other doctors I have appointments with will clean and examine my yellowing teeth, biopsy at least eight possible skin cancers while zapping twenty other spots, take my blood, and feel my body to see how my tumors are growing. By the way, my CAT scan turned out as well as can be expected. The oncologist predicts I'll be back in chemo sometime in 2011, and well past my eighty-fifth birthday in January. Not too bad.

The upcoming free lunch seminars in this ten-day period include a wonderful array of top-notch restaurants. The cuisine is varied—steak, fish, continental, and healthy. I plan to take Herb with me on three of these visits—not for companionship, but as an assistant reporter. I haven't told him as yet. I'm going ask him to sit at a different table at the luncheons so that he can interview other attendees and endeavor to develop material that I can use in this book. He may balk at first, but when I tell him I'm going to mention his name in my book, I'm sure he'll come around. Maybe he'll be a sport and pick up the tip for the valet.

KATZ AND DOGS

It had been raining heavily since yesterday as Tropical Storm Nicole brushed past the coast of Florida. I received a harried call that morning from an employee of the financial group that was sponsoring the evening's dinner/seminar in nearby Boynton Beach.

The caller informed me that because of the expected deluge, attendants with umbrellas would be at the Westchester Country Club to shelter my walk from the parking lot. I realized that her boss was afraid that many/most/all of the invited guests would cancel because of the weather, and that he'd be on the hook for the restaurant's tab anyway. But as you may already have guessed, neither snow, etc., would keep this chronicler from a free dinner— especially at a place I'd never been to before.

Westchester Country Club is a public club and is a relation, in name only, to the one just north of Manhattan. That's the way country clubs are named in South Florida. There's one in Boca named St. Andrews, and the only thing Scotch is behind the bar.

At 5:30 p. m. I bounded excitedly into my dirty car and headed north, off to another free dinner. And on the way, my car was getting washed as I drove through the pouring rain. I always wondered what it would be like if I poured some soapsuds on the roof just before I left the safety of the garage. I'm sure my neighbors would get quite a kick seeing my Batmobile sudsing down the street.

It was just a short drive, and the heavens cleared as I drove. I said a short prayer that the title of this episode (see previous page) relates to the weather forecast and not to this evening's entree. I walked rain-free into the foyer and went through the usual routine of check-in, nametag and receiving my package of promotional materials.

5:55 p.m. Enter medium-sized room with three rows of tables set up facing a projection screen and podium. Man steers me toward a seat in the first row, but head to one in the second row, one seat away from a couple of old ladies (but who are a good bit younger than I am). Never got their first names, but let's call them Alice and Tina. There are place settings for forty or so, but only about half of them have a plate of bruschetta in front of them. Finish off one of these Italian-style open sandwiches before my fanny hits the chair. Too many onions. Eat the second and last one. Glad I'm not sitting close to anyone. When speaker comes over after dinner to ask me to set up a follow-up appointment, I'll breathe right in his face.

Examine my place setting as thoroughly as if I'm investigating a crime scene on CSI Boynton Beach. The silverware is commonplace. Two knives, two spoons, fork, glass filed with water and lemon (portends no iced tea tonight), coffee cup with wrapped mint on the saucer), pat of butter wrapped in gold foil (ingredients, pasteurized cream and salt) and green cloth napkin, all resting placidly on cream-colored tablecloth. Examine stamping on the back of the silverware. Says "Walco." Must mean it comes from Walmart. Plain knife is serrated, but it couldn't cut through steak or roast beef. Chicken, here we come. Hope it isn't too tough.

Speaker paces up and down the room like prospective new father outside hospital delivery room. He's antsy that the rain will keep many people away. Room slowly fills with three sets of two ladies, six couples, and two other singles; it looks forlorn with so many empty place settings, and so does speaker.

6:10 p.m. Alice finishes her bruschetta and longingly eyes uneaten portion between Tina and me. Aggressive Alice nudges timid Tina to take the plate, but she's afraid someone might come and sit there. Wonder if should get the evening's festivities off to a flying start by taking the appetizer right from under their noses.

Soon the waiter ("Manny" on bronze name tag) comes to pick up bruschetta plates from around the room (some empty, some half eaten, some full). Alice grabs nearby-uneaten appetizer out of waiter's hands. They split it (Alice and Tina, not Alice and Manny). Like Alice right away (not that there's anything wrong with Manny).

6:15 p.m. Speaker off and running. He tells us he is a CPA, CFA, CLU, and a ChFC. Says going to speak for thirty minutes. Has already taken up three minutes reeling off credentials. Theme of this seminar is, "Getting Your House in Order." He says investing is on everyone's mind after the stock market crash and recession. Asks audience, "How many hits do you think you get on Google when you search for the word investments?" Guy in front row answers, "Seventy million." Speaker looks flabbergasted. "Pretty close," he replies. "Seventy-two million."

6:30 p.m. Speaker finishes his thirty-minute pitch in twenty minutes. I'll save you the details. Introduces president of the company, let's call him Samuel. Nattily dressed seventyish, shortish, and well spoken. (But he has a sore throat. Hope this means he won't be able to talk very long, and we can get down to business of the evening, eating).

Tells us his firm has been around for twenty-five years and that they have a CPA, lawyer, financial planner, and hairstylist on staff. Maybe he's exaggerating about having a lawyer.

144

Then requests we close our eyes and think of our first job, our first child, and our first etc. When he finishes, we open our eyes, all except one woman who has either fallen asleep or been hypnotized.

His firm offers "Growth Without Risk Through Annuities."

Samuel's basic pitch implies you can receive 8 percent annual income on your investment, 3 percent guaranteed growth in principle, maybe more, and you can't lose original investment. "Sounds too good to be true," he says. I agree. Look around for a grain of salt.

7:05 p.m. Samuel finishes and then walks around the room chatting amiably with each of his guests. Ask for details about the annuity he described, and he responds with all the clarity of a presidential candidate at a nationally televised debate.

Then first speaker comes by, and I ask him to explain it to me in more detail, which he is more than willing to do. Turns out that it's not exactly the way I understood it to be. It's complicated, with more nuances than a TV soap opera. Some of his affirmations are hard to swallow—especially before I've been served dinner—but he did provide some food for thought.

7:10 p.m. Warm bread arrives. I pass. Then, all hail to the Caesar salad. Heavy-handed dressing. No wonder he was stabbed.

First speaker makes rounds to pick up info sheets and try to make an appointment for the complimentary meeting at their office. I write on my sheet that I'm not sure if I want to participate. He reads my note and tells me that's fine, he'll call me.

7:30 p.m. Manny comes back with entrée, chicken with brown sauce, mashed potatoes, broccoli, and carrots. Needn't have worried; my serrated Walmart knife is able to cut the chicken. It's not bad, and since it's past my usual dinnertime, gulp it down.

President of the company sits down to eat dinner with his guests. This is a first. Goes around the room, taking a few bites with each of us. "Great dinner," he proclaims.

Overheard Alice telling Tina that she couldn't follow a lot of the presentation because she left her hearing aid at home. I'm not sure whether she did this on purpose or not.

Lean over and remark to Alice that she didn't finish her chicken. "How was it?" I inquire. She responds, "Menza, menza" (or was it "Mezze e mezze?") while shrugging her shoulders and raising both outstretched arms. Without understanding the words I deduce her meaning.

7:40 p.m. Finish my dinner and wonder if it's worth waiting around for dessert.

Decide to kill time and see what the men's room looks like.

Pass Manny on my way back. Ask him what's for dessert. He tells me it's sorbet. Go back in, and soon Manny delivers a very refreshing dish.

As I get up to leave, I snap my fingers very loudly. The woman who had closed her eyes earlier snaps awake.

I hopped into my newly washed car. An evening well spent.

SOMETHING FISHY HERE

I've been to Bonefish Grill so many times in my adventures that it's like a second home to me. This afternoon I'm scheduled for a 3:00 p.m. seminar, which means dinner will be served a little after 4:00 p.m. I prepared for this by limiting my lunch to two bites of a leftover dish that we had doggie-bagged from a restaurant two nights ago.

As I walked up to the doors of the eatery, I saw two people that I thought I recognized from a previous seminar. The man smiled at me as we passed. This had never happened before. I was very excited. (Not that a man had smiled at me, but that I might have finally come across another freeloader.)

I checked in at the front desk. The "checker inner" was a pin-striped suited young man who took names and then led each person (or couple) to one of the eight tables for four, set up in the main dining room. His forehead was glistening with beads of per-spiration. I wondered what he was nervous about, which made me apprehensive. Either his boss' financial planning or the food was going to be dangerous to my health.

I asked to be seated at the table of the couple I thought I had recognized and introduced myself to them. No, they hadn't ever been to a seminar, but they were an exceedingly pleasant and friendly couple of refugee South Carolinians. We exchanged pleas-antries and background (his was MBA in accounting, same as mine, and then math teacher, accountant, and finally a boat builder in South Florida). I told them that I was working on this book and that I had been to many seminars. Bill asked what I had learned so far. I replied, "Always order chicken instead of steak." They laughed. I immediately took a shine to them.

The menu on the table listed a choice of two chicken dishes and tilapia (my choice). No salad, no dessert. Pretty chintzy. Almost not worth the trouble of coming. Almost.

With this sparse menu I can see why the "checker-inner" was nervous. I envisioned an uprising by the guests, but no one else seemed to be agitated. Perhaps they came to hear the lecture.

3:00 p.m. President of financial planning company is introduced. Well-dressed, barrel-chested orator. Starts off by reading a long legal disclaimer. This is the first time any firm felt the need to do this. Makes me suspicious, especially since I just learned on TV that China is a major exporter of tilapia to the US.

His approach to lecturing is to continually ask "softball" questions of the audience. Attempts to elicit a response each and every time. Gets annoying, like a TV commercial repeated time after time. However, maybe I'm just being petulant; most of the twenty-six people in attendance get into the spirit of things and cry out "Yes!" to every question:

"Anyone been or going on a vacation?"
"Did you have to plan for the trip in advance?"
"Do you want to plan for your future?"
"Is a financial checkup a good idea?"
"Is body odor getting you down?"

To break up monotony, he sometimes asks a question and indicates he wants to a show of hands instead of verbal response. Each of the twenty-six robots in the audience raises hand. Speaker orchestrates them like marionettes.

Notice there is a playoff baseball game on the TV set in the bar that is clearly visible, so tune out his presentation and concentrate on the game. Tampa Bay is playing Texas. Decide to root for Tampa Bay.

To add a little humor to the lecture, he tells this joke:

Boy says to his grandpa, "Please make a sound like a frog." "Why?" his grandpa asks. "Well, Grandma was in the kitchen with Mother, and she said that when Grandpa croaks, we're all going to Hawaii."

Aside from this feeble attempt at humor, I have to say he did have several points of interest in his very professional PowerPoint presentation and that his puffery was minimal. Only wish he had spent less money on his computerized show and more on our lunch.

4:10 p.m. "Give yourself a round of applause," he says in ending talk. All the trained seals get up on hind legs and clap. They rise up and sit back in unison to simulate a wave running through the room, just like the crowd watching the Giants' football games.

4:20 p.m. Tilapia arrives and none too soon. Look for "Made in China" label. Presenter walks around to each table to "make nice." His assistant has been watching the baseball game in the bar and now comes around to each table to set up appointment for a "Complimentary One-Hour Review." I decline. No pressure. My tablemates sign up.

I arrived back home at 4:30 p.m. and dropped into bed. Many people have asked why I take two naps every day. The answer is simple. It's so that when I die, it won't be such a shock to my system.

'TIS THE SEASON TO BE FOLLY

I picked Herb up at 5:30 p.m. and pointed my trusty car south by southeast toward Seasons 52, our target for tonight. I felt the excitement Jesse James must have experienced as he set off, with his brother Frank riding next to him, six-shooter in hand, to pull off another job. I looked over at Herb and smiled. He understood.

The restaurant is noted for a seasonally inspired menu and the promise that no dish exceeds 475 calories. I'm looking forward to a satisfying and healthy dinner in pleasant surroundings, and not having to open my wallet.

5:45 p.m. Pull into parking lot and leave car with valet, figuring Herb will pick up the tab. Hostess tells us the room will not be ready till six. There are seats for six in the foyer, and we take two on a bench for four. More guests flow in and mingle. One flamboyant woman starts chatting with a bench mate and passes her a flyer promoting a singles group meeting on Mondays, for which she is the facilitator. Ask for a flyer. She says I can't have it if I'm married. I protest that it's just for a friend. She doesn't believe me, but reluctantly hands it over. Facilitator pushes her way through the waiting group and passes out more flyers.

The flyer is for over-fifty singles and refreshments are served. Wonder if Judy would let me go so I could write it up for this book. That's a rhetorical wonder.

6:00 p.m. We're herded into a private room in the back. Turns out the shepherdess is leading us to slaughter, because the evening's seminar presentation is the worst I've experienced. (Details will follow.)

Six tables are sardined into a small, noisy room. There are place settings for thirty-four, and eventually about twenty-five show up. The other nine must have had a premonition of what lay in store for them.

Take seats at a table in the back and are joined by John, who impressed me right away because he enters carrying a glass of wine he purchased at the bar. Soon a modern-day Jack Sprat and his wife sit down with us. Introduce ourselves to them. Ask why they are late, and he answers enigmatically, "An emergency." Perhaps his wife got hungry on the way to the restaurant, and they had to make an emergency stop at Wendy's.

Examine menu on table. Wow. Four courses plus coffee. Had so much steak that I order chicken, as does Herb. John has the fish, and Jack and his wife order steak. (Did you know that the limerick about Jack Sprat originated in the 1600s? The first recorded lines are shown below.)

Jack will eat not fat, and Jull doth love no leane.
Yet betwixt them both they lick the dishes cleane.

In the rest of the episode, will refer to our tablemates as Jack and Jull.

6:30 p.m. Platters of flatbread arrive, followed by late-arriving host. He (let's call him Frank) tells us he got lost, even though he has held several seminars in this restaurant. This is a harbinger of things to come: he has trouble operating the computer for the PowerPoint

151

presentation, and can't get Muzak turned off. Ray Charles is soulfully belting out, "Georgia on My Mind."

Frank shakes hands and hands out packets to each of us. My packet is empty (figures). He laughs and gives me another. Nothing in the material describes his company. Later on informs us that he and his agents have ten thousand clients and that his firm has offices in several states. Wonder how he finds his way to these offices.

6:35 p.m. Starts his presentation, inexpertly using his computer to key the images on the screen in front of the room. Can't hear him, and people complain. If had known what a confusing and boring speech he was going to give, we would have asked him to turn the music louder. Finally I get up and turn a switch on the wall, and the music is off. Become a folk hero, like the Dutch boy who stuck his finger in the dike.

Frank is a pleasant guy, and sure he knows his stuff; he's just not well organized, well prepared, or well anything. Presentation is geared toward people who have a net worth in the stratosphere.

Speaker discloses he lives in Miami and drives to his office in Boca each day. Ask him why he doesn't have office in Miami, and he replies, "I don't speak Spanish!" (The busboy hace un gesto de bochorno.) He follows that bon mot up with a story of how, at a previous seminar, one man asked, "I have ten million dollars to invest. Can you help me?" Frank said several single women got up and joined his table. Polite chuckle is all he gets for his efforts.

Frank says long-term health policies are worthless. Better to buy a life insurance policy via a loan and use cash surrender value if you have big medical bills in future. Who knows?

Speaker declares that stock market shouldn't be going up because of weakening economy and high unemployment. Asserts the reason for the Dow zooming is that institutional investors can borrow money from Federal Reserve for less than one quarter of 1 percent and buy stocks with it. They use these mega-millions to buy stocks and drive up market. Then one day they are going to all sell their stock and reap tremendous profits. Then they'll all short the market, and the selling pressure will drive the market down, and they'll make another bundle. Wonder what he smokes. Could use a puff. Wouldn't inhale.

Says 96 percent of all life insurance policies lapse.

Jull (you may remember she's Jack's wife) rolls eyes in disbelief and whispers to me, "He's overtired and punchy."

7:28 p.m. Frank starts talking about another subject. Asks, "Anybody hungry?" People at next table start rhythmic applause to try to get Frank to pipe down and have dinner brought out. Applause sweeps room; crowd on the verge of getting ugly? If Fletcher Christian were in the audience, he would have led another mutiny. Captain Bligh is impervious to the unrest and starts talking about annuities." Finally relents and says, "Thank you."

"You did a helluva job, Frankie!" some Democrat shouts, mimicking George W.'s comments to FEMA director after Hurricane Katrina struck New Orleans. (If he were a Republican, he would have shouted, "You did a helluva job, Baracky!" to recognize his BP fumblings.)

7:38 p.m. Salad served by Sophia, our waitress. Very tasty (the salad). Jull eats half and gets the rest to Jack. Their platter is cleane.

To pass time ask Jack what he does for a living. Tells me he's sixty-nine and retired; collects bonsai plants, says has nine hundred. Jull says, "No, you have 890." Ask what he did before he retired, and he avoids answering my question. Jack is thin and sallow-complexioned. I conjecture he is a recently released felon.

8:00 p.m. Entrée finally arrives. Gobble it down. Good food.

8:30 p.m. Waiting for dessert. Specialty of the house. Decide to pass (fattening). Tablemates Jack, John, and Jull are pleased. They can have our desserts, and do. Bid farewell to new friends. The singles group facilitator is still giving out circulars.

Herb offers to pay tip for parking and slips me $2. Make a feeble attempt to refuse. Pocket one of the singles (to apply against the gas).

8:40 p.m. Jesse James and Frank get back into the car and speed away. Mission accomplished..

PS. I forgot to mention that Herb turned down my offer to become an assistant reporter. He said he's not cut out for that line of work. Herb flinched slightly when I asked for his badge back. If it weren't for the fact that he picks up the tip for valet parking, I'd drop him like a hot potato.

ADDENDUM: Do you know that there are two definitions for the word glutton? (1) A person who eats and drinks excessively or voraciously, (2) And a person with a remarkably great desire or capacity for punishment.

Well, I'm ambidextrous, because both #1 and #2 apply to me. What else would you call anyone who learns of a future seminar hosted by Frank, the same speaker you just read me describe sardonically, and who thinks of accepting because it's being held at The Cheesecake Factory? I'd love a shot at a slice of their chocolate peanut butter cheesecake. The expression "To die for!" is apropos.

But I've adopted a "Don't ask, I won't go" policy, which means that even if some company invites me to go to their seminar for a second time, I won't attend.

A MELLON RIPE FOR THE PLUCKING

Q. What do you get when you mix one of Wall Street's largest trust companies with one of Boca's finest steak emporiums?
A. A beautifully cooked eight-ounce filet mignon as the centerpiece of a three-course luncheon fit for an Earl.

That's what happened yesterday when I feasted at The Capital Grille, courtesy of BNY Mellon. And, oh yes, I did have to sit through almost two hours of a sales presentation about estate planning and investing. I'd rate the meal three stars and the seminar no stars. Listen up, and I'll fill you in on the details.

I put my car into autopilot, and it took me to Herb's house. We then set sail for The Capital Grille for our 11:45 a.m. seminar. The hungry duo was early; the trim, black-sheathed hostess proffered us a seat in the bar.

11:45 p.m. We are escorted by the tight-fitting dress to a private dining room at the back of the otherwise-empty restaurant. Very classy, expensive-looking surroundings. If Obama raises taxes on the rich in 2011, wonder whether anyone will be able to afford to eat here.) [Promotional consideration has been received from the GOP.]

Private room is exquisitely furnished with (1) five white tableclothed-tables adorned with gleaming silverware, and (2) an equally gleaming six-foot, dark-haired woman who represents BNY Mellon's Private Wealth Management—Boca division. Decide to transfer my brokerage account to her on the spot.

Pick up silver pen at my setting and use it to check off my lunch selections, which are: salad with shrimp, eight-ounce filet mignon, and fresh fruit cup for dessert. By now am a connoisseur of the free lunch circuit, and can assure you that at every other seminar, the filet was always six ounces or smaller.

First fly in the ointment makes its appearance when a small, thin man with sneakers and no socks takes his seat at the next table. Hope he doesn't see me and spread the word that I'm freeloading.

Salad with shrimp on top is served. Appears to be four small shrimp. However, on closer inspection, it's only two shrimp cleverly and precisely cut in half and duplicitously placed face up on the salad to look like four. Bet most guests thought they were eating four crustaceans. (Second fly in the ointment.)

12:00 p.m. Introductory welcome speech followed by top-notch lawyer who talks for half an hour. Don't understand a word he was saying, but it sounds important. (Third fly...)

12:45 p.m. Director of portfolio management proves to be fourth fly in the etc. Great charts on screen and in material in our packet. Predicts market will be up another 4-5 percent by year's end. Spoils it all when he recommends gold, but doesn't know symbol for the ETF. When Herb asks the inane question, "I have $500,000 to invest. Can you recommend an investment that will yield 10 percent and be relatively safe?" the guy says yes.

Four waiters and busboys are continually going in and out of the room, serving each course, pouring water, refilling glasses with soft drinks and more water, bringing a fork here, a spoon there. See Ray, our waiter, taking notes during the talk on estate planning. Either that or he was writing down the dark-haired woman's phone number.

1:15 p.m. Main courses arrive. Spokesperson says, "We'll take a five-minute break for lunch." Steak is cooked perfectly. Not sure I can finish it and the sides within five minutes. Gulp the feast down within the prescribed time only to find that "five minutes" was only a figure of speech. Need Tums when get home. The guy from my community gets up and leaves before dessert. Wonder what he knows that I don't, but eat my berries with relish.

1:45 p.m. Spokesperson says thank you and collects evaluation sheets and the form with which to ask for a future appointment. Herb and I throw away our forms and beat it out the door.

We plucked the Mellon all right, seeds and all, and I have two more free lunches later this month at The Capital Grille

FRANCHISE OPPORTUNITY FOR MY READERS

I've decided to cash in on my newly acquired expertise in the field of free lunch seminars by franchising. I've hired a recently laid-off executive at Burger King to direct this operation. With so many people monitoring their pocketbooks very closely these days, why wouldn't they want to be able to put a big dent in their food budget? And for those husbands who can't stand their wife's cooking, here's a subtle way to get them out of the kitchen. As Henny Youngman said, "My wife dresses to kill. She cooks the same way."

I promise the franchisees that:

They will eat out free of charge at least two times a week. They will eat at fine restaurants they never would have dreamed of dining at. They can impress their friends by mentioning where they ate last night. They will learn how to sit through a boring two-hour lecture on any number of subjects without going stir-crazy. They will learn how to disguise their voice and appearance so they can keep going back to the same sponsor's seminars over and over again. We will provide, at a slight extra charge, kits with mustaches, fake noses, and wigs. They will learn how to covertly bag up and take home food that is placed on the table for people who have already left the seminar. They will learn how to forge driver's licenses and passports so they can attend those seminars for which they might otherwise not qualify because of strict age restrictions. They will learn how to write a book about their experiences and earn a huge profit. They will have an exclusive territory of fifty miles from their home.

And, if you sign up in the next ten minutes, I'll include my pamphlet on "How To Fake Choking on Your Food at Your Favorite Restaurant So You'll Receive a Free Dinner for Everyone in Your Party." You can invite a large group to Ruth's Chris Steak House for your next birthday and not have to pay a red cent. Guaranteed.

LEGAL DISCLAIMER: Earl Bronsteen Franchise Unlimited Inc. is not liable for monetary damages, physical harm, pain or suffering, medical expenses, or loss of pride caused by your attendance at any seminar, including, but not limited to: heartburn or food poisoning, valet parking tips, fraud, and emergency room foul-ups.

ALL THIS FOR A LOW DOWN PAYMENTOF $100

PLUS SHIPPING AND HANDLING $15

BUT WAIT, I'LL INCLUDE A SECOND FRANCHISE ABSOLUTELY FREE

JUST PAY SEPARATE SHIPPING AND HANDLING

STRICT LIMIT OF 100 FRANCHISES PER EXTENDED FAMILY

MY FREE LUNCH COST $115

One of the strangest ads for a free lunch seminar appeared two weeks ago. It was a full pager and was topped with the headline:

THE UNITED STATES IS ON THE VERGE
OF A DEVASTATING FINANCIAL MELTDOWN
LEARN WHAT THE BUREAUCRATS
DON'T WANT YOU TO KNOW

The name of the sponsor was not included in the ad, but since lunch was free and served up at a wonderful restaurant, Brooks, I called and made a reservation. Herb saw the same ad and joined me. The day before the lunch, I received the obligatory confirmatory phone call. But this time the caller told me that I'd have to bring a picture ID. Maybe there's a statewide crackdown on double dippers.

11:30 a.m. Arrive at the appointed time (present our IDs) and are led into the main dining room, which was set up with nine tables.

Tablemates are three single older women, a couple (man and wife) and a forty-five-year-old black man. In all the seminars I've attended, this is only the second time that an African-American was present.

The first thing always do after sit down at a seminar is to examine the silverware and try to guess what we are going to be served. Wow,

160

am almost blinded by the array of silverware; three forks, two spoons, one knife and a coffee cup, blue water glass, and a napkin; salad and dessert are a slam dunk.

No menus in sight. Waiter arrives and asks us to choose between chicken and salmon. Everyone makes his or her selection save the woman (Dorothy) on Herb's right, who inquires if the salmon is farm raised or wild. Waiter responds, "Wild." She continues interrogation. "Are you sure?" Waiter answers in the affirmative and stalks off. (Don't you just hate it when you answer someone's question and they reply, "Are you sure?")

Herb asks Dorothy, "What difference does it make if it's wild?" She pulls her nose up and responds haughtily, "All the difference in the world. Farm-raised salmon are crowded into pools and they mutate." Herb gets into the spirit and inquires, "Can you tell the difference between the two species by looking at them?" "An expert can," is her retort. Wonder is she is a member of ASPCFF (American Society for the Prevention of Cruelty to Fish Farmers), but decide to let sleeping fish sink.

11:45 p.m. Very pregnant receptionist greets us and reads a lengthy disclaimer (not about absolving her boss for her pregnancy, but about no matter how many lies her boss tells, he's not liable). Says examples in the presentation are hypothetical and may not resemble actual results. (Want to shout "Amen," but restrain myself.)

Speaker enters. He's a PhD in finance and economics, war veteran, Life Insurance Million Dollar Roundtable member, national speaker and frequent guest on TV and radio programs. Very impressive, nice manner.

His message is twisted. On one hand he's Cassandra ("Chicken Little" to my non-Greek readers) predicting a financial meltdown (stocks, bonds, gold, treasuries, and real estate are not safe); on the other hand he's Gordon Gekko preaching that everyone should own some of each of them. Then says he still likes gold; he bought in at $800. Likes diamonds. Tells us his mother escaped from Germany with the family's wealth converted to diamonds.

Says public company execs are still crooked. The market is going up because they are touting their company's fortunes and soon will sell. Gives strange example to illustrate his point.

12:10 p.m. PhD asks if he can loosen his tie. Keeps asking softball questions to keep audience involved. Gets good response. With a three-course feast coming, who wouldn't be in a receptive mood? He asks, "Can you buy a hamburger with gold?" "No" resounds through the room, but no one seems to know just why you can't.

Asks, "What do you buy if stocks look bad?"

"Bonds," echoes the Jewish chorus. (There weren't any Greeks in the audience.)

Asks, "What do you buy if stocks look bad?"

"Real estate," everyone answers.

Asks, "What do you buy if real estate looks bad?"

"A gun!" man answers, catching the heretofore-unflappable speaker by surprise.

12:40 p.m. Woman asks if you have to pay income taxes if you sell gold at a profit. Speaker responds, "You are supposed to," with a wink in his voice.

12:50 p.m. Presentation ends. We talk among ourselves. Sam and Sarah are a seventyish couple. Engage them in conversation to develop material for this story. Before the presentation she had told me, "You can't believe anything they tell you at these seminars. " Her hubby had nodded in acquiescence. Asked her why she had come—she gave me a Mona Lisa.

After speaker finishes his hour-long presentation, Sam is all smiles. He declares, "The speaker is the best I ever heard. He tells it like it is." Sarah beams in agreement. And what, you ask, made them both change their minds so completely? It's a prime example of human frailty. Whenever someone's opinion matches your own, you respect that person. We only want to hear what we already believe. That's why conservatives tune in to Rush Limbaugh. (I tune in to Sesame Street.) Enough homemade psychoanalysis.

The irony, as far as Sam and Sarah are concerned, is that they only heard what they wanted to hear. Sam's net worth is all in cash. He's bearish and scared. He thought the PhD had given the same bearish advice, but he hadn't, even though at one time or another he seemed to tiptoe on both sides of any issue. Try to point out that their assessment of the speaker's words is not accurate; I make two enemies with one sentence.

1:00 p.m. Chicken, tomato confit, rice, and four thin asparagus spears. Very tasty. Dorothy seems to be enjoying her wild salmon. If she only knew how the waiter had doctored her fish before serving it, she wouldn't be so pleased. Everyone licks his or her platter clean, except for married couple, who call for a doggie bag. Busboy does a landslide business in passing out tin-foiled trays (for later).

1:30 p.m. Apple tart with vanilla ice cream. Only eat the fruit. Herb asks for my ice cream, as he did for my roll. Coffee all around.

1:45 p.m. Pregnant greeter comes to each table to pick up info sheet to see who wants to set up future free consultation with the PhD. Estimate about two or three people from each of the nine tables sign up. None from our table. Woman to my left is already a client and says she is very happy with his performance. Herb and I say our good-byes and leave.

We got back in my car and headed north toward Boca. I noticed a police car in the next lane and kept my speedometer pointed at a safe twenty. All of a sudden I hear a siren blaring on the police car, whose lights are now flashing. I pull over, at a complete loss to understand why I'm being stopped. A polite policeman asks for my registration and license and goes back to his vehicle for about five minutes. I wonder if he has read the pages in this book that relate to my childhood indiscretions. He returns and informs me that my tags have not been renewed since 2008. I say that's impossible because I've always paid every bill I've ever received on time. He looks at me with a knowing look on his face (knowing I'm eighty-four). I search in vain through my cluttered glove compartment and can't come up with a receipt for 2009 or 2010. He hands me a yellow traffic citation that carries with it a fine of $115. For that money I could have taken Judy to Brooks, had a fine bottle of wine and Dover sole—and not have had to listen to another interminable lecture.

I am sure that I never received any notice from Motor Vehicles, impossible, as that may seem. There's no earthly reason for me not to have paid it—and to miss two years in a row is inconceivable. I may be eighty-four, but I was only eighty-three last year. I'd like to fight this in court. I'd offer to take a lie detector test. But when the judge takes one look at my grey hair and considers my age, I'm sure he'll determine that I had two senior moments, one year apart.

I've been driving around without a current registration tag for twenty months, and I get picked up on a day I'm hitting a guy up for a free meal. There must be a moral to this episode, but I'm not sure what it is.

PS. I spent two and a half hours at the Motor Vehicles Bureau waiting in line to get my tags renewed. I told a woman behind the desk that I had never received any renewal notices. She said the envelopes probably got stuck together in the mailing process, but anyway it was my responsibility to renew. I paid up, with a penalty included in the charge. At age eighty-four, I'm still learning.

HEAVEN PRESERVE US

I noticed an advertisement in the local paper placed by The Preserve, a retirement facility. I was skeptical at first, because the name sounded to me like it might be an "embalming factory," but I continued reading the ad:

"What better way is there to welcome in fall than on Wednesday, October 13, at noon, at our fabulous Harvest Fest? Enjoy flavorful fall food…"

I didn't have to read any further and placed a call to the number in the ad to flesh out what "flavorful fall food" means. I really wanted to attend this seminar because I was sure that the food would be amazing. I reckoned The Preserve wanted to impress visitors with how wonderful their cuisine was, since a resident would be eating there for the rest of his or her lives. A vision of sitting at the table, like the one in the Saturday Evening Post cover by Norman Rockwell, laden with turkey, stuffing with chestnuts, cranberry sauce, and pumpkin pie came to mind.

When I called to preserve my reservation, Nancy answered. I wanted her to think that I was old enough and infirm enough to need to move to a retirement community, so when she asked me where I lived, I replied, "Boca Raton."

She asked, "Where in Boca Raton?" I replied, "17543 Lake Estates Drive."

She asked, "Is there an apartment number or suite number?"

I replied, "No."

She asked, "Is it in a gated community?"

My reply was, "Yes."

She asked, "What is the name of the community?

I paused awhile and then responded, "Can't remember."

She replied, "Hurry on over."

On October 13 I set off for the half-hour ride to welcome fall in at The Preserve. The place was easy to find. All I had to do was follow the cars with "disabled" license plates. Mary greeted me at the foyer of the main building. She seemed surprised to see me. The preserve had placed ads in three newspapers, and only ten people responded; and of this number only three showed up for their fabulous Harvest Fest (their words, not mine).

11:30 p.m. Mary points out a few dreary points of interest, including the main dining room of the independent living facility (the assisted facility is next door). "We are going outside to a pavilion, where the buffet lunch will be served," Mary announces. Sniff the air, but can't smell the turkey roasting; guess we were too far away.

Mary also informs me that there will be live entertainment, just as promised in the ad, and it's an accordion player. Ask if we can skip the accordion player, and she replies, "I see we have another jokester."

A short walk brings us to another dining area sparsely decorated with fall ornaments. The fifteen or so tables were occupied by residents—mostly older women, many of whom had a three-wheeled walker, cane, or battery-operated cart by their side. It was so depressing that I almost lost my appetite. Little did I know that would have been better off if I had.

Mary tells me to join the buffet line, help myself, and take a chair at any of the tables. Musician (he's the one on the right) serenades me as I move forward in the line. Later on realize never took notice of what songs he had played.

Lawrence Welk would have loved the entertainment.

"What would you like to have?" the pleasant lady asks when I get to the head of the line. "What are my choices?" I respond. "Knockwurst or bratwurst," she answers. What a way to welcome in fall. Can you imagine the Pilgrims being greeted by Squanto on Thanksgiving with the query, "Knockwurst or bratwurst?"

Chose one, can't remember which, embellished with potatoes and onions on a richly decorated paper plate. Their chef sure pulled out all the stops to impress potential residents. Sit at an empty table and enjoy my feast. Put a can of diet soda in my pocket, for later. Glance down and observe that had forgotten to zip up my fly. No one seemed to notice or those that did, didn't seem to mind. Maybe it's not so bad here after all.

Mary comes back and asks if I'd like to see one of the rooms. She takes me to the second floor to see a neat two-bedroom apartment, which rents for $3,000 per month. It comes with two meals per day and once-a-week maid service.

We pass an elderly man in the hallway and get to talking. Tells me he comes from the Bronx and that he had been a "bookie." Pursue the subject, thinking there might be an interesting story here, but after awhile he admits he was kidding. Another jokester.

I beat it out of there and hope I never have to come back. It's hard to imagine what the assisted living section is like. Reminded of Thoreau's comment, "The mass of men lead lives of quiet desperation."

And then they wind up in a retirement community, munching on bratwurst to celebrate fall. What a way to go.

PS. What a dummy I am. I have to eat humble pie for making fun of The Preserve because they observed fall with bratwurst instead of turkey. They were celebrating Oktoberfest, not Thanksgiving. I should have realized that at a predominantly Jewish residence facility, they'd pull out all the stops to commemorate a German holiday.

GOOD NEWS AND BAD NEWS REDUX

"How was your dinner seminar?" Judy asked as I stepped in the door at 7:45 p. m. *"It was terrible,"* I replied irately.

I feel like ending my description of this episode with those words, but that wouldn't be fair to my readers, so I'll fill you in on the heart-wrenching details.

I had made a reservation to go to a seminar at the Boynton Beach Jewish Community Center. The subject: "Staying Heart Healthy." I had trepidations about going on two counts. First the ad said that a "Light dinner would be served." And even worse, there was to be a $2 charge. I've almost never paid for it in my life and I had reservations about starting at age eighty-four, but I had an opening on my calendar and I went.

The good news was that they never charged for the dinner, which consisted of a half tuna wrap, half egg salad wrap, miniature cup of coleslaw, and chocolate cookie all elegantly crammed into a white Styrofoam takeout container, plus your choice of warm soda, hot coffee, or ice water.

The bad news was that the original physician, whose topic was, "Staying Heart Healthy" couldn't make it. One of my tablemates wise-acred that the doctor probably was held up in court defending a malpractice lawsuit. Another heart doctor stood in for him and gave a technical one-hour talk (with slides) dealing with hospital procedures for people who had attacks. Most of the sixty or so seniors in the audience didn't seem to mind. I would hazard a guess that many/most of the attendees were a missed heartbeat away from dialing 911.

In the Q&A that followed I asked him what I should do to stay heart healthy. He laughed and said that would take an hour's lecture. I couldn't complain that I had paid good money to attend to get the answers to that question, so I just pointed to the ad in the paper. He retorted, "That's what the other doctor was going to speak about." Then he told me to eat fish, not red meat*, to exercise, and not to eat things that were white—no pasta or flour dishes.

I realized the doctor didn't want to give the audience any information about how to prevent heart attacks because that would kill his business. He had sixty live ones living on the cusp in the audience and attending to their heart maladies would pay for an awful lot of tuna wraps.

As I pulled my car out of the parking lot, I passed an EMS vehicle heading in the opposite direction.

    *   His comment about not eating red meat just added insult to injury. I've got several seminar dinners lined up for this month at Boca's top steak houses. Now I'll have to order fish. Ugh! Maybe I'll go for a second opinion. There's another seminar next week at the JCC titled, "Heart Health From A to Z." It costs $2 to get in, but if this doctor recommends eating steak instead of fish, it will be worth it.

HOLY MOSES

I've finally paid for it. No, not for my sins, not for a hooker, but for an "almost" free lunch seminar. I kicked in $2 at the JCC to get into a lecture on "Heart Health from A to Z," with lunch included.

This historic episode started at 11:30 a.m. on October 21, my eldest son's birthday. When I opened the door to the large meeting room at the JCC, I had to wade through a sea of Jews—and when the waters parted, I found a seat at a table for ten. I escaped completely dry, that is until a woman sat down next to me, and in doing so clumsily doused me with coffee (decaf). I toweled off with a paper napkin and went over to the table where our lunches were stacked and packed in white Styrofoam takeout containers.

The nice lady behind the counter asked for my name, and since I was not a member of the JCC, she said, "That will be $2." I asked her, "Will you take $1.50?" We settled on $2.

I took my booty back to my coffee-stained table and opened it. Since the lecture dealt with a "healthy heart," it was more than a little surprising to find half an egg salad wrap, ditto for tuna salad (both slathered with mayo), and a chocolate chip cookie. This was the very same menu we had been served a week earlier at another JCC seminar. The coincidence went even further. The chocolate chip cookie looked familiar. Last week I had not eaten mine and put it back in the box.

This was the very same cookie! I recognized it because I had put a little dent in the cookie when I took a taste. I felt a momentary feeling of elation—much like that of the young lad who put a message in a bottle and cast it upon the waters, only to find it washed up on a faraway beach ten years later.

But I'm sure you're much more interested in what the physician told us about keeping our hearts healthy. His prescription in a nutshell: eat veggies, fruit and nuts, cut down on salt, stay away from trans-fatty acids, exercise, take a baby aspirin daily, have good genes, and see your doctor regularly.

Outside of the nutshell he gave us two other hints: (1) don't ever try to take your pulse by putting a hand on your neck—you can cause a heart attack, and (2) it's OK to take generics, if they seem to be helping, but tell your pharmacist to fill each prescription *from the same manufacturer.*

The doctor told the story of a pharmacist friend of his in India who took back to the US samples of one very popular generic drug that had been filled by five different Indian manufacturers. The lab here reported that one of the samples contained 95 percent of the ingredients it was supposed to and that all the others only had 70–80 percent of the required dosage. (I guess the other 20–30 percent was made up of "pill helper.")

The other highlight of the seminar, at least for me, was when a woman in the audience asked what was in the clear red plastic heart-shaped souvenir she had received? (There were about fifty tiny white pill-like tablets in the container.) He answered, "They're mints." Everyone smiled. You ask, "Why was that the highlight of the seminar?" Well, the same woman had asked the same question a week earlier at the previous seminar. She was seated at the table on the right, just behind the plant. "If that was the highlight of the seminar, what was the low point?" you ask audaciously. "Almost everything else," is my response.

The grey-haired woman with her back to the camera
is shown passing a 'nosh' to her friend (for later).

WHAT HAPPENS AT THE MARRIOT...

I received the strangest phone call. It was from one of the men associated with the financial services company that had provided me with a free lunch at Bonefish Grill a month or so ago. He invited me to another seminar that his firm was holding in two nights. I had seen their large ads, but had ignored them because of my policy not to hit on any sponsor a second time in the same calendar year. (I have a high set of standards to uphold in an otherwise dirty business.)

It's also the company run by someone who lives in my community, but whom I've never met.

I told the caller that I appreciated the invite, but that I've already been to one of their seminars. He said, "That's quite OK. My boss will be there, and he's a very entertaining speaker." I hesitated because all they were serving was hors d'oeuvres, but I was anxious to see Harold in action.

I accepted his invite and decided to take this as a personal challenge. Could I turn an offering of hors d'oeuvres into a full-blown dinner? If, in 1579, Stephen Gosson could write of, "seekinge too make a silke purse of a Sowes eare," why couldn't I do the same some five hundred years later? (I like to add a tad of highbrow erudition to an essentially lowbrow book.)

I arrived at The Marriot for the seminar promptly at 6:00 p.m., only to learn that the seminar was scheduled to start promptly at

7:00 p.m. I checked my calendar book—sure enough, the scheduled time was 6:00 p.m.—but for a different seminar at The Marriot four days later (another senior moment).

I trudged back from the ballroom to the lobby and took a seat, wondering what I was going to do for the next sixty minutes, and on an empty stomach, no less. Forty-five minutes later a group of ten people took chairs right next to me. They were all greeted warmly (hugs and kisses) by a man in a suit and tie whom I guessed (correctly) to be one of the salesmen at tonight's seminar. He fetched bottles of water for them while they waited for the doors to open. The group of friends was plainly garbed and spoke with the intonation/accent of Italian Americans. I didn't catch their names, except for the first name of one man they all deferred to. His name was Donald; I couldn't catch his last name. They kept referring to him as Don. Their mien and banter reminded me of a scene from *The Sopranos*. I was immediately ashamed of myself for making this characterization, but just to be on the safe side I'm going to sit with my back to the wall in the dining room.

Well, I seem to have strayed a bit from my story about tonight's episode. A huge sign in the lobby promoted the seminar, headlining that over forty thousand people attended these seminars in the past year and a half. They use newspaper ads and mailings to chum for investors. I wondered how many were freeloaders.

7:00 p.m. Join a line to sign in and receive my table assignment (#19), which is the furthest away from the podium of the twenty-four large round tables set up in the ballroom. (While waiting in line notice that five large rolling buffet tables, each bedecked with a panoply of appetizers, are being pushed into a room some thirty yards away from the ballroom.)

Take a chair at table #19 but got right up and beat a hasty, stealthy advance toward the room where the buffet is served. No one else is there! Walk in and feel as if I am starring in a Fellini movie. Move in a trancelike state from counter to counter, putting one hors d'oeuvre in my mouth for every one put on my plate (well, really two plates; they are small). The chow (rhymes with sow, and that's what the hors d'oeuvres are mostly all about—bologna, salami and prosciutto slices) looks appetizing, but it will take quite a lot to make a meal out of these bite-sized morsels. Go to each of the five stations and load up plate and stomach. Walk back to #19. Tablemates ask where I got the food. Tell them. Off they go. Back they come with plates loaded with cheese, cold cuts, and veggies.

7:10 p.m. Couple on my left converse in a foreign language, which I don't recognize. Ask the husband what language he's speaking. "English," he replies indignantly. Tell him had overheard him speaking in another tongue. He tells me, "Oh, that's Portuguese, and my wife only speaks Spanish. She doesn't understand Portuguese." The logic of this escapes me for the moment, but imagine that's the reason they've been married for such a long time.

He tells his wife not to have her coffee now, but to wait to have it with the dessert that's always served at the end of the seminar. Seems to know his way around. It turns out he invested in one of Harold's REITs two years ago and that he's very happy with the check he gets each month. It represents 8 percent per annum of his investment. Wonder if the 8 percent is in Portuguese. Tells me he just came for the free food. Advise him that I saw an ad for another one of Harold's seminars next week at which they are serving dinner. He's upset that he missed it and tells me he'll check his old newspapers. Maybe he includes the value of all the free meals he and his wife garner in computing his 8 percent return.

Wonder how come two hundred people turn out for a lecture featuring just a snack, when most of the seminars I've attended that offered steak dinners had only twenty in attendance.

7:30 p.m. Harold takes the mike. He's short in stature, maybe five foot eight, but when he stands on his wallet he's six foot four. A real rags to riches success story—from the south Bronx, to a summer residence in Long Island and a winter home in Boca Raton. Speculate that the apartment he grew up in would fit comfortably into one of his wife's closets in Boca. Got to give him a lot of credit.

Harold spends the next two hours telling about his company and its products. It's the same story I heard at the previous seminar at Bonefish Grill. Wonder why I was personally invited to attend tonight. Guess that each of the fifteen salesmen had a quota to meet.

Harold used to be a high school teacher and he handles the audience as if they were in his classroom. No one is allowed to talk or move around. One couple gets up (to go the bathroom as it turned out) and he makes a comment that they are "eating and running." No one else dares get out of his chair for the rest of the lecture. Anyone caught not paying attention is in trouble, with a capital T.

His voice alternates between a whisper and a gravelly shout. He's a born entertainer and loves being in front of an audience. Bounds around the room like the Energizer Bunny. He's got panache (entusiasmo in Portuguese) written all over him.

Harold tells us that at the end of the seminar there will be a drawing for a TV set and other gifts and that dessert will be served—which also serves to keep all two hundred people strapped in for the duration.

Begins PowerPoint presentation. First slide shows his company's paradigm. Always wondered what that word means, and until I got home to my computer, I never knew. (Merriam-Webster: an outstandingly clear or typical example or archetype.] Won't bore you with the details of his paradigm.

Says customers have invested $6 billion in his real estate deals since 1993. He grosses 10 percent or $600 million, equal to $35 million per year.

9:20 p.m. Lecture over. Great applause. Believe almost everyone in the audience would like to become an investor if he could. That's how convincing he is. Dessert is served. Brownies and chocolate chip cookies. Wonder if the cookie from the JCC could possibly have followed me here. Portuguesan/American neighbor is upset that the dessert is so shabby. Not too upset to wrap up a handful of brownies and cookies. My kind of guy. Wish I spoke Portuguese.

Some people leave but most wait for the drawing. Harold's salespeople go from table to table attempting to make appointments. Torn. Should I leave because it's almost past my bedtime and am very tired or will my name be on one of the tickets pulled out of the raffle drum? Sure I'll be a winner, so stay. Since I hadn't been able to reach my son, Richard, on the phone before I left to wish him a happy birthday, turn on my cell phone. It was dead. Had forgotten to charge it. This is my second senior moment.

Didn't even win one of the two $4 umbrellas offered as prizes. Left about 9:30 p.m.

I pulled my car into the garage at home some twenty minutes later and found a harried Judy walking into the garage from the house. She berated me in an angry voice, "Where have you been? I was worried sick when you didn't answer your phone. I called the hotel and they said the seminar was over at 9:00 p.m."

I explained that the hotel had given her the wrong information, and that most people remained for the dessert and prize drawing. I wondered why The Marriot hadn't used more discretion. The operator should have had the sense to say that the seminar was still going strong, i.e., "What happens at The Marriot stays at The Marriot." Judy declares, "Don't you ever go out without having your cell phone charged. I was sure you had an accident driving home." I calmed the little woman and dropped exhausted into bed.

As I lay on my pillow I remembered a story Ray (a tennis-playing friend) had told that morning. He's a born jokester. It's very apropos of the last segment of my evening.

"I wasn't feeling well last night," he said, "so Ellen went out to dinner with some of her friends. She didn't get back till 4 in the morning. I asked her what took you so long." Ellen replied, "The service was very slow!"

THE THIGHBONE IS CONNECTED TO...

I told you it I would happen again. Lightning struck the second time in Boca when I went to see a spine surgeon—the very one whose seminar I had attended at the local deli. This marked the second time I had been so impressed by the presentation at one of my free lunch seminars that I subscribed to or became a patient of the sponsor.

And In my very first office visit, the spurgeon (combo of spine and surgeon) cleaned up enough to pay for the cost of the fifty or so coffees and mini-Danishes he had so generously provided at the seminar I had attended.

As is *de rigueur* when you go to a physician for the first time, you have to fill out page after page of info about your medical history. It took quite awhile to answer all the questions. While I did this a woman sitting behind me was having trouble with her form. The conversation went like this: Wife: "Do I have tingling, burning, pins and needles?" Husband: "I don't know what you've got." Wife: "All I know is it 'hoits.'"

A nurse who went over the info sheet I had filled out saw me. Then they took five X-rays. Then one doctor saw me and went over the same info and did a physical exam. Then the spurgeon came in for a few minutes and scheduled me for an MRI. (I wondered if he owned a piece of it.) Then the nurse scheduled another visit in two weeks with both doctors. I could hear the cash register ringing.

EXPLANATION OF MEDICAL TERMS:

Don't confuse the word *spurgeon* (a spine surgeon) with "sturgeon" (a delicious fish when smoked and served with a smear of cream cheese on a bagel and topped off with capers).

You don't need a surgeon to debone a sturgeon, but the spurgeon would probably take five X-rays first.

DAY 1

It's Monday morning, October 25 and I have a busy week ahead, with four seminars in the first three days. This will help me keep my mind off Election Day, November 2. The Democrats are going to lose control of the House (and maybe the Senate), and I'm going to lose the fast-growing tumor in my left armpit. My oncologist decided that the results of my last CAT scan made him want to have my largest tumor removed and biopsied. The operation will require anesthesia, and the surgeon said the growth was in a delicate place. After the surgery I won't be able to use my deodorant under my left arm for a while. I'll have to keep my friends on my right. At my community most already are.

Tonight at 6:00 p.m. I'm due back at The Marriot for an evening of appetizers, drinks, and an exclusive presentation by a well-known economist.

6:00 p.m. Walk into lobby and pass the free drink dispenser. This week it's cranberry sangria. Very refreshing. Turns out to be the highlight of the evening. Check in and am name-tagged. The covered open-air pavilion is my home for the next three-quarters of an hour.

Here's a first. There's an open bar serving wine and beer. Too bad I'm a teetotaler. Hot appetizers are few and far between. Tough to make a dinner out of chicken on a stick, raspberry cheese balls, micro-scopic pieces of beef, and the ever-present veggies and cheese.

Strolling waiters with their puny platters attract the serious eaters as bears to honey. The rapacious guests sagaciously position them-selves by the door so they can pounce while the getting is good. I always beat them out.

Not enough chairs. The young people don't mind. Sit on a cement ashtray receptacle while lying in wait for the bayoneted chicken appe-tizer to push through the door.

6:45 p.m. It's too warm outside and I'm tired from all the stand-ing and appetizer chasing, so go inside and find a few other alter-cockers (old folks) resting comfortably in the air-conditioned meeting room. One sits next to me with his wife. Complains about the heat outside. Complains he wore a jacket and tie because, "When I go to a nice place, I try to dress appropriately. Next time I'll wear shorts." (I'm the only one in shorts in the whole crowd.) Complains that you can never believe anything the government tells you. Unemployment and business are much worse than they let on. Tells me that Nathan's and Arthur Treacher's restaurants closed at the big mall in Sawgrass.

7:00 p.m. Room slowly fills up to about 70 percent of its 160 capac-ity. Many seem to be employees or customers of UBS, the sponsor. Men running the seminar can't get the PowerPoint system to work. Seems UBS changed its passwords last week and there were problems in the translation. (Strike one.)

7:15 p.m. After brief introduction of the Wealth Management Group running this seminar the speaker is introduced. Characterizes his phi-losophy as to the right of Attila the Hun. Says if you're a Democrat or a Liberal, you're not going to like me. I don't think Attila would have liked him. (Strike two.)

Very supercilious. Seems like a "My way or the highway" type of boss.

Says CNBC is "The Brady Bunch on Crack." Always playing up the worst.

He's very bullish on the stock market. Says everyone should buy stocks because stocks always go up after they go down. Wonder if he told everybody to sell stocks when the market had gone up, "because stocks always go down after they go up."

People start deserting the room as he smugly drones on and on. This flight becomes a mass exodus during their "well-known economist's" talk. His theme: buy stocks, "It's not as bad as it seems." He's conservative also. Tells the crowd that TARP was a big mistake and so was the stimulus, but for some reason AIG's bailout was good.

8:10 p.m. Shows a slide that I consider in bad taste. It shows one man's solution to stopping BP's oil spill in the Gulf. Picture depicts the White House, turned upside down, being lowered into the waters to plug the leak. Guess it all depends upon whose ox is being gored. (Strike three.)

8:20 p.m. Can't take it anymore and head for the exit. Pass the cranberry sangria dispenser. No paper cups. Figures. Am very thirsty. There are a few paper napkins on the table, and I consider opening the spigot onto the napkins and then squeezing the cranberry-soaked paper into my mouth. Attila wouldn't have minded.

I headed home, still hungry.

DAY 2

At 5:30 p. m. I headed for The Capital Grille for another dinner seminar, courtesy of UBS. It's as if UBS wanted to make amends for last night's double-edged disappointment, when the food and the speeches left a bitter taste in my mouth. I was sure that last night's fiasco wouldn't be repeated, because an entirely different division of UBS was sponsoring this seminar, and The Marriott can't hold a candle to The Capital Grille.

6:00 p.m. "Red or white?" are the first words I hear as I take a seat at a rectangular table set for twelve in the same private room I've come to almost regard as my second home. "Iced tea," I respond to waiter in as blasé a manner as I can muster. Want my hosts to understand that I am not impressed by ostentation and it will take more than a glass of wine to win over this freeloader.

Waiter offers tray of filled wine glasses to couple seated next to me. "Red or White?" he intones. "They're playing our song," husband smiles to wife.

A seventyish woman comes in outfitted in black and Tiffany (the $1,400 an ounce variety). Recognize her as the person who sat next to me at a seminar two months ago. We had chatted and found that we had once worked for the same Wall Street firm, but at different times.

I had confided to her that I was writing this book, and swore her to secrecy.

She extends her hand to me in greeting, which wasn't as easy as it sounds, with all the jewelry weighing down her protrusion. Breathe a sigh of relief—she doesn't recognize me. Not so good for the ego, but plenty good as far concealing my identity from my hosts. Turns out she's a client of the hosts, a very satisfied one. We table chat for a few minutes and then I turn to view the other guests. One man's nose looks familiar, but can't place him. He and his wife are with another couple, and there's a nondescript couple at the other end. Wonder how they'd descript me.

Several seats unoccupied. Woman walks in and host tells her to sit anywhere. She looks around and realizes she's in the wrong room and exits. Hosts seem disappointed.

No menu anywhere to be seen. Never had that before. Look under the table. Host asks what I'm looking for. What could I say? "My pen," I respond.

6:30 p.m. Both hosts speak about stocks, bonds, etc.

7:00 p.m. Speeches end. One host sits on my left and tries to make nice. Asks if I play golf or cards. "Tennis," I reply. He asks, "What do you do for fun?" I break into a spontaneous laugh. How can I tell him, "This is what I do for fun."? Couldn't think of an appropriate answer that would make him happy, so just sit there and try to look like an old man who's happy to be breathing regularly.

Fried calamari served. Ugh! Salad. Better.

Just then the woman in black across the table claps her hands together and says, "I remember you. You're the one writing the book about…" I interrupt her and hold a finger to my lips. "Please don't say another word," I admonish her. "If you try to unveil my identity, I'll have to kill you." She catches herself and promises to withhold my secret. I'm not sure how long she's going to be able to keep my secret; she can hardly contain herself because of the incredulity of the coincidence. It's a bit like a comic opera.

Other host sits down on my right. Sandwiched between the two hosts—between a rock and a hard place. Can't take any more notes, so everything that follows is from memory.

One of the male guests starts conversing with lady in black. Finds out she's divorced and wealthy; she finds out he's living with some-one, he's wealthy, and innocently flirtatious. He mentions he lives at a nearby community, one where Judy and I used to live. A light bulb goes off in my head. I ask the man he's sitting next to if he lived there also—and he says yes. Turns out he was captain of the tennis team I played on for many years, and that his friend became the partner of the fellow I had played with as a partner for many years. "What a small world." we all say.

7:40 p.m. Steaks arrive. Family style. Pick up T-bone in my hand. Delicious.

I wondered what tomorrow would bring.

DAY THREE

Q. What is the cost of the tolls on the Florida Turnpike from my home to the Devonshire Life Care Retirement Community?

A. $5.

Q. What is the cost of the gas to make this round trip?

A. $15.

Q. What is the cost of having lunch at Devonshire with an eighty-six-year-old pixie, a seventyish Italian American widow, and an Argentinean-born wife of a Miami physician?

A. Priceless!

Ethel, Terri and Gloria join Earl for a free lunch.

The thirty-six-mile trip to Devonshire in Palm Beach Gardens took thirty-five minutes on the Turnpike. I left my car with the valet and was led into the dining room. I was told to sit anywhere and made a serendipitous decision to join Ethel, Terri, and Gloria. Over the course of the next two hours our diverse quartet bonded together as strangers rarely do. The sponsor's representatives talked about the merits of living at Devonshire ("It's considered the crème de la crème") and of the superiority of their food ("Our chef is from The Yale Club"). We talked among ourselves, sharing experiences and feelings.

Gloria will be eighty-six on January 15 (three days before my eighty-fifth). She started the conversation by saying that I looked familiar and she thought she had seen me at another assisted living community. Her mind twinkled in and sometimes slightly out of reality. She was cognizant of her frailties. "I'm going to change my name to Devon Shire," she announced. "That way if I live here, I'll always be able to remember my name."

Gloria was a slow eater and had hardly touched her salad when the waitress came to pick up the plates. She asked for a box so she could take it home. A woman told her that they were not allowed to let guests take food out of the dining room because it might spoil, and Devonshire would be liable if the guest took ill. Gloria said, "Well then, I'll finish it," and proceeded to slowly do so. Then she exchanged her salmon main course for pasta, but was too full to take more than a few bites.

She told us that two people from her church had moved to Devonshire and they didn't like it here. I realized she was a kindred freeloader.

I'm sorry I didn't take a picture of Gloria's fingernails. She showed me her hand and asked me if I noticed anything unusual (meaning the ghastly green nail polish). I told her I noticed her rings. She replied with a smile, " Oh no, they're not real diamonds. Look at my nail polish," proudly holding up her hands. "I got it at a seminar I went to."

Terri related how difficult it was for single women to travel alone. On a recent cruise she was in the movie theater when a stranger "footsied" her. Gloria got up and complained to the purser and was pleased to report that from then on there was always someone from the crew nearby. I wondered why she had repulsed her would-be Lochinvar without as much as smelling his feet.

When Terri heard me tell how quickly I had made the trip from Boca, she said I must have driven with a "heavy foot." As I was leaving, she told me to be sure not to speed on my return trip.

Ethel came to this country from Argentina when she was quite young. She came to this seminar on behalf of an aunt, who will soon need to move into such a residence.

After dessert, I told my tablemates that I had a secret I wanted to share with them. I whispered that I was writing a book about my adventure at seminars. Gloria remarked, "That's why you've been taking so many notes. I knew something was up, because none of the speakers had said anything worth writing down."

I told them I'd send a copy of the photo we had taken with my camera. Ethel gave me her e-mail address; Terri gave me a card with her name (and her deceased husband Lou's name) on it. Gloria wrote her address on the back of her nametag. (I hope she'll invite me to her next birthday party.)

As I was getting up to leave Gloria slid two Splenda packets into my papers. She had seen me use Splenda for my iced tea and was presenting me with a going-away gift or a memento of our meeting. I was very touched. I was reminded of the quote, "Age cannot wither her, nor custom stale her infinite variety."

As for the luncheon itself I was most surprised how many of the twenty or so seniors acknowledged that they had been to a lunch at Devonshire before. I wondered if I had run into a swarm of Palm Beach Garden's freeloaders.

The speaker brought her presentation to an end with these words, "The rest of our life needs to start as soon as possible." Our Gang of Four was doing its best, each in his or her own way.

The valet retrieved my car and refused my extended dollar bill, saying, "Tipping is not allowed." A perfect ending to a perfect luncheon. I only wished I had tried to tip him with a fiver.

I drove at a moderate speed back to Boca to get ready (by taking a nap) for my evening dinner seminar. When I entered the house, I found a note from Judy saying that she'd like to accompany me to The Capital Grille at 5:00 p.m. for the financial services seminar that evening. I was dumbfounded. She had told me many times, "I'd rather be dead than go to one of those things." I later found out that she had swung 180 degrees because this would have been the third night in a row she would have been alone for dinner, and my mouthwatering description of Capital Grille's steaks was the last straw in overcoming her resistance.

So arm in arm we entered the hallowed halls of one of Boca's steak heavens—and this was less than twenty-one hours away from when I had wiped the last trace of Capital Grille's chocolate cake from my lips. We were ushered into a different private room, albeit smaller.

A week before the seminar the financial guy (let's call him Edgar) who was running the seminar called. He wanted to meet me *before* the seminar, and he wouldn't take no for an answer. He was trying to weed out the freeloaders, I guess, but I explained I would only attend a group meeting. Edgar was really pissed off, but finally agreed to let me come as an "uncommitted" guest. We got off on the wrong foot, and he stayed on that leg during the seminar. Thirteen of us were squeezed in around a circular table that took up most of the space in the room. (It wasn't the sponsor's fault; one couple arrived who had received a mailer invite but who hadn't called to register.) Four of the guests were new clients. One couple was Judy's bridge buddies, but fortunately they hadn't learned about my working on this book about seminars. She surely would have spilled the beans.

A frumpy, almost hobo-like guest turned out to be a psychologist who was writing a book on various activities of the brain. He told us he disliked living in his gated community because all the residents thought about was bridge, tennis, and golf—no intellectual stimulation. (I guess he hasn't been able to find the XXX-rated channel on his TV cable guide. It's #832.)

The table was so cramped, I didn't have room to take notes, so the following account of the evening's happenings is from memory—and my short-term memory is unreliable, so none of what I've described below may have actually transpired.

5:15 p.m. Edgar welcomes us and apologizes for: (1) last-minute change of the seminar to 5 p.m. from 5:30 p.m., which was occasioned by the restaurant's booking of this room for another meeting at 7 p.m.; (2) crowded table, and; (3) late start of the presentation. Most of speech is spent recommending adjustable-rate bank loans, an arcane investment vehicle that provides higher yields in an increasing rate environment, but with greater risk.

Touts his ability to invest in stocks, bonds, etc. ("I don't work for Morgan Stanley; I work for you.") New clients agree that he has done a good job for them. Of course they're riding the wave of a strong stock market, but what the heck, the dinner is free. He can say whatever he wants.

Because of time restraints dinner is served during his presentation. Judy gets her heart's desire (tournedos), but I order chicken.

He talks; we eat: he talks; we eat. But while Edgar is talking, one of the women (Marion) at the table asks neighbor to "please pass the mashed potatoes." *Edgar almost blows a gasket. She had had the temerity to put the importance of getting some spuds ahead of listening to every one of Edgar's pearls of financial wisdom. He stops mid-sentence and storms to a corner of the room, where he finally composes himself with the aid of a swig of water. No one besides the two Bronsteens seem to notice his fit of anger; they are all too busy eating the delicious fare. Marion hashes the mashed.*

In the Q&A Judy asks Edgar what was the yield to date of his stock fund. He spends the next five minutes explaining how he had made money for his clients by selling covered calls on a particular stock, and then he asks for the next question. Duh.

Unless Edgar is able to pull a rabbit out of his hat within the few remaining minutes, his tournedos of goose is cooked, as far as getting Judy and me to consider him as our investment advisor.

6:45 p.m. Manager of The Capital Grille is getting antsy about our group's not evacuating the room with enough time to clean and reset the table for the next private group. He swings both of the doors wide open, which brings the seminar to a close. (Don't rush. Here's your hat.) Wonder if we could stay in our chairs and join the second seminar— like going to a movie in a Multiplex theater and sneaking into a second picture. But instead we gracefully exit.

Summary: Edgar may well be an excellent financial advisor; we just didn't find the chemistry right for us. We both felt he should continue in his anger management program." Two days later Edgar called to try to turn me from a freeloader into a paying client. He had an edge to his voice, as he felt me slipping away and in desperation mentioned that he had spent a lot of money on our dinner.

I said I thought that the firm that packaged the bank loans had picked up the tab. "Oh no," he declared. "I did. I'll show you the credit card receipt." I thanked him and said I'd call if I was interested. I thought I heard his phone crash into the wall just before the line went dead.

DAY FOUR

I didn't have any more seminars planned before my surgery on November 2, but I did have a return visit scheduled with the spine surgeon to review the results of my MRI.

At 3:15 p.m. the doctor's associate (an MD) saw me, asked the same questions he did last time, poked my body, looked at my file to see "who the hell I was," and told me the head honcho would be right in. The surgeon appeared and said he had reviewed the MRI and wanted to inject steroids into my spine. I reminded him that last time he thought that arthritis in my left hipbone was causing the problem and that injections in my hip would be beneficial. He dismissed my comment and then added that I needed to get an MRI of my neck. I asked him why he hadn't had the neck MRI done at the same time as the previous MRI he had ordered, but no answer was forthcoming.

Then I asked him if it was OK for me to have these injections in my spine today, as I had lymphoma and was having a tumor removed on Tuesday. He was stunned and said of course I couldn't have these injections and that he would never have suggested it if he had known. I told him the info about my cancer was in the file I had filled out and which had been reviewed by his nurse and the examining doctor. I don't know if he had ever looked at my file. I felt like saying that if he spent a little less time giving seminars all over town, he'd have enough time to read my file and learn about my case.

He told me to have a neck MRI and see him in six weeks. I told him—well, I would like to have told him to shove his MRI up his a _ _, but I just stormed out. He couldn't have cared less and raced out to see his next patient. All I got out of these visits was some unneeded radiation from the X-rays.

PS. Listen to these coincidences. Herb went to listen to the same doctor at another of his many seminars at Poppy's Restaurant. (It was packed.) Herb made an appointment even before he finished his mini-Danish and visited the doctor the same day I did. A technician took five X-rays. The surgeon then spent the better part of four minutes with him, paying little attention to the detailed files Herb had brought with him. The doctor told Herb to take two MRIs and "come back in the morning."

When the MRI clinic called to set up the appointment, the surgeon had prescribed they ask Herb if he had a pacemaker (yes) and a stent (yes) and then told him because of that he couldn't have an MRI. So Herb had to call the surgeon's office and make a new appointment. Keep tuned.

A week later: After more tests and another four-minute meeting, the surgeon told Herb he wasn't a candidate for surgery because of his advanced age and since he wasn't in such dire straits. Why this wasn't apparent on Day One remains a mystery. I guessed Herb had aged a lot in a week. He recommended Herb take a series of physical therapy sessions from one of his staff.

All the tests and X-rays were just a waste of the government's money (as would have been the expensive MRI). Herb took back his files, which evidently no one had ever bothered to look at.

DOUBLE DIPPING NEAR THE OCEAN

I headed for the Boca Raton Resort and another free meal. This would be my first seminar at this famed resort, and since BNY Mellon was the sponsor, I was expecting quite a banquet to celebrate my return to action.

Yes, I know I promised never to go back a second time to any one sponsor's program (so that I could spread the pain around), but I had an excuse. The first BNY Mellon seminar was co-sponsored by a law firm, so it only counts as a half. And today's seminar is co-sponsored by a life insurance agency, so two wrongs equal one right.

Here's what transpired today. I pulled my car into the posh Boca Raton Resort and left it with one of the five valets waiting to get their hands on the guest's cars. I used the words "get their hands on" because there was a bronze plaque announcing that the parking charge for guests was $10. I thought of pulling my car right out and settling for a Big Mac for a buck—and I'd have $9 left to do with whatever I wanted, but I figured I had a fifty/fifty chance of still getting my money's worth.

The meeting room was at the far end of the hotel. It was a long, arduous walk. I was back in the saddle, but where was my horse when I really needed him?

The room was quite large, with seven resplendent tables set up with six chairs facing a large projection screen. Two men manned the audiovisual equipment.

12:00 p.m. Have some more good news and some more bad news. The good news is that our hosts are picking up the $10 parking fee.

The bad news is that I am cut off at the pass as soon as I sit down. The tall moderator I told you about at BNY Mellon's previous seminar comes up to me, glances at my nametag, and says, "Hello, Earl. You've been here before. I have quite a few customers not only in your community, but on the very street on which you live." How do you respond to that greeting? Try to think of an appropriate answer—maybe tonight something will come to mind. Sure she'll be calling to follow up and put some polite pressure on me (like the threat of mentioning to my neighbors that I am an habitual freeloader.)

With my cover blown, almost lose my appetite, but not quite. (The meal consists of a salad, a chicken dish, and a fancy chocolate dessert. The iced tea comes with a sprig of mint.)

Two men sit down next to me. One looks familiar. Turns out he lives in the same community where we used to live. His name is Gluckstern. Whenever a Jew from New York hears the name Gluckstern, he immediately thinks of the famous deli on Delancey Street. My tablemate says he is a distant cousin of the pastrami maven, which makes him quite a celebrity at our table.

A young man in a suit and tie comes over and says his father is one of the speakers and that he saved Donald Trump $5 million on his insurance premiums. Want to respond that if his father had saved me $5 million, I'd have $5 million, but decide not to make waves inside such a nice dry room."

You're not interested in what the two speakers have to say about stocks, bonds, and life insurance, so let's move on to the highlight of the luncheon. After the meal is finished, the man on my left takes out a small matchbox (with the name of his country club emblazoned on its cover) and offers me a toothpick. Judy would have died, because she hates to see people pick their teeth in public, but I think it would be impolite to refuse. The three of us pick the remnants of chicken, greens, and chocolate from our teeth with the gusto and élan of The Kingston Trio.

It's good to have clean teeth again.

POTPOURRI

Well, I was finally back at Abe & Louie's restaurant to get my revenge. You've forgotten, but I haven't. It was almost exactly two months ago that I attended a luncheon seminar at this great steak house and ordered hamburger because I misread the menu and couldn't find steak on the bill of fare.

11:00 a.m. Enter the restaurant and am led back to the same private dining that was "the scene of the prime" sixty days earlier. Amazed to see only six other people in this spacious, mahoganied room. Randall, the Wall Street investment advisor/sponsor of the luncheon, doesn't even have an assistant. Says there are usually eighteen to twenty at his seminars. Blames it on the fact that it's Monday. Can't figure out what that has to do with anything, but I hone in on the proffered menu. There it is on the third line—Steak and Tomato Salad. I'm home free, but wait, there's a fly in my salad.

Look up and recognize one of the speakers. He happens to be a lawyer whom we once used to prepare our wills, but we left him many years ago. He used to live at the same club as we do, but after a messy divorce (a redundancy), he moved away.

Haven't spoken to him since; we just don't travel in the same circles. Embarrassed he'll recognize me and ask why we haven't used his services again. On edge all meeting long but he never recognizes me. Perhaps because I have lost so much weight, or that now parting my hair on the right, or that I'm just that forgettable. Whatever the reason, he is plenty pissed that he has come to this seminar to address only seven people. When it is his turn to speak (about estate planning), he talks disinterestedly for perhaps five minutes and then beats a hasty retreat. Did have time to mention he has been married for twenty-five years; didn't have time to mention that he included back-to-backs.

Despite the slim crowd think the main speaker picks up two clients. Somehow feel I contributed to his success by just being there.

My cell phone rings. Embarrassed. Judy wants me to pick up groceries on my way home. Can you imagine Bob Woodward's wife calling him while he's interviewing "Deep Throat" to give him a grocery-shopping list? Tell Judy we have a bad connection and hang up.

Sit with a middle-aged couple who came from Lake Worth. Guess they are fellow freeloaders to have traveled that far.

12:15 p.m. Lunch is served. Steak is delicious. Beefsteak tomatoes with bleu cheese and special steak sauce are as good as I could have hoped for. No dessert and no appetizer, but what the heck, the price is right. (You know the old saying, "Be careful what you wish for..." When I got home had a tummy-ache. Don't know if it was the bleu cheese or if the attorney had somehow gotten the chef to spike my food. Can't use the expression, "He got his just desserts." Because there wasn't any.)

1:00 p.m. Speaker finishes, packs up his computer and papers, and rushes back to his office. Turn to my tablemates and try to lure them into a conversation in order to develop something interesting to write about so that this episode wouldn't be a complete dud. Tell them that I used to be an artist and that writing a book about free lunch seminars. Bella is amazed at my revelation—not because writing a book, but because became an artist late in life. She had been an antique dealer on 47th Street in Manhattan and when they moved to Florida six years ago, she started to create art. She excitedly starts to tell me about her work.

Then Bella asks me, almost apologetically, if I am Jewish. When I answer in the positive, she grows quiet. Her face becomes expressionless, and she tells me she is a Holocaust survivor. I am stunned because of her Italian surname. Bella says she had married an Italian, but that he had a "Yiddisher kop."

When I tell her I am interviewing people that meet at these seminars for my book, she begins to pour out her life story, starting with her birth in 1945 in Siberia. What a way to start a story. Learn that in mid-1939, as the drums of war could be heard in the distance, that many Polish Jews decided it was safe to stay put and not flee, but not Bella's grandmother. She told her two daughters they were to get married the very next day (to their sweethearts) and then they all fled to Siberia before daybreak the following morning. Hitler invaded Poland in September 1939. Only twelve of her two hundred close friends and relatives survived. Bella draws a deep breath and asks if we could continue outside, as "I need some fresh air and a smoke." She laughs quietly at the incongruity of her statement.

We spend another ten minutes talking outside and then go our separate ways.

WHAT YOU HEAR IS NOT WHAT YOU GET:
YOU CAN'T TOUCH WHAT YOU SEE

The first caption above describes all of the many seminars about annuities I have been to since starting my eating binge odyssey on May 25. None of the speakers lie, but they use smoke and mirrors to camouflage the full story about the annuities they are hawking. (I'm not knocking annuities. Millions of people were better off having their money in annuities than in the stock market the past ten years.) They are complex instruments, and I doubt that most purchasers fully understand what they've bought. And usually commissions are on the high side.

The hour-and-a-half presentation at the seminar I attended last night at City Fish Market was no exception. The crux of the evening was epitomized by a brief exchange between George (our sponsor and the speaker) and a woman in the audience. He had given an example where, over the course of several years, the original value of $100,000 a hypothetical customer had invested with him in annuities had grown to $150,000. At the same time, in his example, if the customer had invested the same amount in the stock market, it would still be worth only $100,000. "Which would you rather do? Invest with me and have $150,000, or invest in the stock market and have $100,000?" Everyone around the table called out, "Invest with George!"

Everyone, that is, except for one little old lady who raised her hand and shyly asked, "Can you take out the $150,000?" George was taken aback and had a look on his face that must have mirrored Julius Caesar's when he turned and saw Brutus raise his knife to deal the fatal blow. I could just see a similar thought going through George's mind, i.e., "I paid good money to rent a private room in a lovely restaurant and provide a wonderful dinner for this woman, and she cuts me to the quick with a knife in the back." (*Et tu,* little old lady?)

George stammered out an answer of sorts. I don't know how many people in the audience realized that the correct answer is you can't take the $150,000 out.

My main complaint about the evening was that I had to sit there starving from 6 p.m. until almost 8 p.m., when my entrée was served. George can say whatever he wants as long as he feeds me in a timely manner.

The speaker was a strict disciplinarian and announced at the very beginning that if anyone had to go to the bathroom, they should go now or forever hold their piece. (No, he didn't use those exact words—I just couldn't resist.) He neglected to tell his guests he'd be talking for well over an hour and a half. Sometime during his lecture two people had to go tinkle and attempted to slink out. They withered slightly under his reproachful glance. The scene looked like a TV commercial for Flomax.

Other important facts: A goodly number of the twenty-five in attendance had been born in Brooklyn. The group ran the gamut from doctors to schoolteachers to a tool-and-die maker to real estate salespeople.

At 7:00 p.m. George realized that his audience was losing their patience about going hungry. The room was glass enclosed, and we could see everyone else in the restaurant eating. He kept repeating, "We're coming down the homestretch." He said the same thing at 7:15 p.m.

Finally at 7:35 p.m. Simon Legree relented and ended the lecture. He made an appeal for his guests to sign up for a free one-hour complimentary review. A riot was prevented when the salad and bread finally made it down the homestretch.

George's assistant then went around the table like a wrestler and tried to pin each of us down to an appointment. I had written on my form that I would call them if I was interested. She didn't want to take no for an answer and tried several times to sign me up for an appointment. I didn't mind. That's her job. My job is to say no.

"We're coming down the homestretch." This time it's me saying these words to you, my readers. I gulped down my salad and chicken in ten minutes, finishing at 8:09 p.m., and asked the waiter if there was any dessert. Upon learning his negative reply I headed for the door.

I wonder if you remember that at the very beginning of this episode there were two captions. Have you been wondering all this time what the second caption, "You Can't Touch What You See," means? On my way out I passed a vast array of fish, including lobster and stone crabs, resting rather uncomfortably, I would imagine, on ice. No, that isn't the answer to the riddle, because the vast array of fish could be touched. The answer is in the next paragraph.

Let's move on to the reception desk where I decided, as I usually do, to ask for a menu to take home as a memento. The young hostess stationed there had cleavage that reminded me of my last visit to the Grand Canyon. She bent down to select a menu from beneath her desk and then handed it to me. I asked her if I could have another menu. She just smiled.

I gave the valet a tip when he drew my car around. He didn't say thank you. I wished I could have the dollar back, especially when I spied a couple from the seminar walking to get their own car from a nearby lot.

YOU CAN PLAY BALL WITH OPPENHEIMER

When I accepted Oppenheimer & Co.'s invitation for a luncheon seminar on November 10, I had no idea that it was being run by the same group of investment advisers who had managed a luncheon seminar three months earlier. I realized my mistake as soon as I entered the ultra-modern 501 East Restaurant on the grounds of the ultra-chic Boca Raton Resort. There stood the same gentleman who had called me after the first seminar to ask if I wanted to schedule a one-on-one meeting with Oppenheimer's people. It wasn't that I had said no that worried me. It wasn't that I was double dipping that worried me, because both of the seminars were paid for in part or full by different outside mutual-fund managing firms. It was that, for some reason, when he called, I decided to tell him what I thought was wrong about the way they had presented their program. I was well intentioned, but I haven't met the person yet who takes criticism well.

"Ball One!" (That's the opposite of Strike One.) The guy didn't recognize me. Whew!

"Ball Two!" (That's the opposite of Strike Two.) The guy who sat down at my table, and only two seats away, was the same man who sat at my table during the previous lunch. He didn't know me from Adam. (Eve probably would have made the same mistake and given me the apple.)

"Ball Three!" (You know the drill.) The young lady (Vicki) who sat opposite me is the one who keeps a record of the invitees and who calls to confirm. I'm not wearing a nametag, and I only gave my name as Earl. I disguised my voice for the length of the entire meeting to make sure she didn't recall our having spoken twice. She asked if I had a cold, but I said, "No. It's just an allergy."

"Ball Four!" There are so many empty seats (ten) in the forty-six-seat private dining room I realized that they would probably have paid me to come so the tables wouldn't look so empty. I learned from the thirty-six-year-old Vicki that each of the no-shows had been contacted the day before and had confirmed their coming. I told her I thought it was disgraceful that anyone would make a reservation, confirm, and then not show up. She could tell I was a straight shooter. She squeezed my hand in appreciation. (No, Judy, I'm just kidding.)

12:00 p.m. Seminar begins with platters of guacamole and crispy calamari passed around. Waiter takes my order for a heavenly hamburger (so much for my vow of abstinence from red meat) and crunchy coconut pie for dessert.

Speaker says there are three goals for today. Only got as far as the first goal, but I'll list all three:

Have a great meal.

Gain at least two insightful pieces of knowledge.

Schedule a meeting and review of your muni bonds.

Did gain two pieces of insightful knowledge. First, the hamburger is so delicious that you don't have to put ketchup or any sauce on it. Second, the chocolate s'mores cake is better than the coconut pie, and am able to arrange a tax-free exchange.

Bye, bye, coconut pie; I was gone in the blink of an eye.

"YOU'RE TOO OLD, I'M NOT BUYING YOU DINNER"

Eliot Schultz, president of Schultz Wealth Management (pseudonyms), angrily spat these words at me at 6:01 p.m. on November 11 at Maggiano's Restaurant. I retreated before his withering glance, careful not to turn my back on him, and exited the restaurant. After being unceremoniously drummed out of his seminar because of my age, I wondered if I should go for a facelift, or at the least some booster Botox shots.

Let me start at the beginning. Upon receiving an invitation in the mail, I called to make a reservation for Schultz's seminar on, "Avoiding Common Mistakes of Investing." The mailer indicated that this meeting was best suited for investors between the ages of fifty and seventy-five. I made a reservation figuring that even though it was "best suited for those under seventy-five," I wasn't so old that I couldn't benefit from some good stock market advice.

I arrived at the restaurant a little before 6 p.m. and checked in at the desk. The woman asked for my driver's license and scrutinized it carefully. Then she gave me a packet of info, told me how to fill in several forms, and told me to sit anywhere. The private room looked forlorn. Only two tables were set up with place settings, and these only for six or seven people. I sat at one and said hello to the couple already seated.

Then the receptionist called me outside and asked to see my driver's license again. She eagle-eyed it and told me to return to my seat. I was barely settled in when she called me again and said I'd have to leave. I asked why, and she replied that when I made the reservation, I had said I was born in 1936, not the 1926 showing on my license. I assured her that I knew when I was born and that she must have written my date in error. She pointed to Mr. Simon, who wheeled toward me and uttered those famous words, "You're too old. I'm not buying you dinner!"

You don't have to feel sorry for me. I called Judy and joined her and our regular Thursday-night dinner partners at a restaurant right around the corner that doesn't have any age restrictions.

I felt sorry for Eliot Schultz. He had tried to attract a big crowd for his seminar by offering a free meal at a fine Italian restaurant, and only a few couples had accepted. (I wondered if he had the restaurant doggie bag the twenty-some-odd uneaten meals he had to guarantee.)

Whatever the cause, Eliot's words and actions were beyond the pale.

I used the expression "beyond the pale" just so I could tell a story about my mother's escape from Poland over one hundred years ago. The word *pale* means a stake or a pointed piece of wood, and an area enclosed by a "paling fence" was considered safe. Catherine the Great created a "Pale of Settlement" in Russia in 1791 in which it was relatively safe for Jews to live. The purpose was to restrict trade between Jews and native Russians. Anti-Jewish sentiment was high in Russia and Poland for centuries, and *pogroms* (destruction of a town) were common.

My mother was born in a small town outside of Warsaw. Her parents were very poor, but the family managed to survive through the generosity of Mother's uncle, who owned the local tavern.

He treated the Polish troops, who were stationed nearby, to free drinks and in return he and his family were kept out of harm's way. My grandfather migrated to America by himself, and then after he had established himself in the sweater business, he sent for the rest of the family. Anti-Semitic feelings were elevated at that time around Warsaw. My mother and grandmother were smuggled out of Poland hidden under bales of hay on a cart ostensibly bound for market. They settled in a section of Brooklyn that was "within the pale." And I live within a gated "pale" in Boca Raton. Many (maybe most) of Boca's residents are Jewish. As a matter of fact the area is so Jewish that even the few churches in town have a *mezuzah** on their front door frames.

* A piece of parchment inscribed with verses from the Torah, which is placed within a small case.

CAN YOU TOP THIS?

You had to have a lot of money to get a free meal on November 16, 2010. The first seminar I was invited to that day, which included lunch at Café Boulud in Palm Beach, was only for those with minimum investable assets of at least $5 million. (No big deal for me, bro).

The "steaks" were raised, so to speak, for a dinner seminar at The Addison in Boca. It was only for those families with investable assets of at least $10 million. (And to think that just two days ago I took a friend to lunch at Sweet Tomatoes, using a 15 percent off discount coupon from the regular $8.99 all-you-can-eat price.)

After getting thrown out of a dinner seminar last week because I was too old, I wanted to take every precaution to make sure I looked the part for these high-net-worth meetings. The only concession I was willing to make in my attire was that I would change my underwear, but what could I do to hide my 2006 Toyota Matrix. It's bad enough that the car looks every bit its $18,000 cost, fully loaded. The car is subject to a nationwide recall because of a faulty acceleration pedal. Suppose when I left the car with the valet at the posh Brazilian Court Hotel (which houses the restaurant in Palm Beach), it zoomed off into the bushes, careened off a Brazilian, and came to rest in the outside dining court? Perhaps I'd better park around the corner, even though valet parking is complimentary. I wondered how much you tip a valet in Palm Beach.

I hadn't been able to take my morning nap before my epicurean expedition to Palm Beach, because every time I was about to doze off, I'd get a vision of a different one of famed chef Daniel Boulud's signature dishes. Perhaps he'd serve quail stuffed with fresh figs and prosciutto, or maybe sirloin burger with short ribs and foie gras, or at the very least spice-crusted tuna with aioli sauce or squab with cherry compote. I left in high spirits for my culinary odyssey, but sleep deprived.

11:45 a.m. Arrive at the Brazilian Court Hotel. Plenty of parking available on the street, but there is a two-hour limit. Wonder if can safely get in and out within the two-hour window. Tough call. Flip a coin. Park at valet.

Led to a beautiful private room. Greeted warmly by business-suited young men. Take a seat at one of the three tables set up with six place settings. Surprised they don't have an overflow crowd for a free lunch at one of Palm Beach's most famous and elegant eateries. Gets worse. Only about half of the seats are finally occupied, and I would guess that half or more of those in attendance are customers of the firm.

Kurt (head of UBS's Palm Beach Wealth Group) tells us to start on our salad. He's stalling, hoping more people will show up. Never happens. At my table I wind up sitting between a corned beef sandwich on rye and a cucumber sandwich on white bread, minus the crust (A rough-around-the edges senior from Great Neck and a society Palm Beach matron with an estate in Scotland. The only things they have in common are big bucks and a strong dislike of Obama.) The Great Necker is a customer of UBS (and several other Wall Street firms). He's not too happy with UBS's performance.

12:15 p.m. Introductory remarks.

12:35 p.m. Entrée arrives. Cold chicken slices lying contemptuously atop salad greens. A forgettable dish. Michelin must be turning over in his gravy. Sure I recognize some of the lettuce in the salad. Know one piece of lettuce looks pretty much like another piece, but swear I saw this very leaf earlier on my plate when the waiter cleared the first course.

The only one in the room for whom this is not a salad day is Kurt, who keeps wondering why more potential customers don't show up. (I surmise that since the weather is so beautiful, the Society "swells" who had a minimum of $5 million to invest were either tooling around in their Rolls Royces or out on their manicured lawns embroiled in a wicked game of croquet.)

Keep drinking cups of straight coffee to fight off my sleep-deprived state.

12:50 p.m. Kurt continues his presentation. While talking he stares intently at each guest for what seems like an annuity. Seems to be concentrating on me. I become transfixed and cannot look away. Wonder if he knows I changed my underwear.

At one point he gave vent to his innermost feelings. "I'm amazed that there aren't one hundred people in attendance at this luncheon, with all the uncertainties in the world and in the stock and bond markets right now." Feel sorry for him. He's one of UBS's top advisors. Pays for an expensive lunch at a swanky Palm Beach eatery, makes a mass mailing, licks maybe two thousand envelopes—and no one gives a damn.

1:35 p.m. Presentation ends. Dessert arrives. Ice cream on a bed of lettuce. No, I'm kidding. No lettuce.

On the way out I met another guest who also came from Scotland. She also was a customer of UBS. The corned beef sandwich was waiting for his car at the valet. I prayed that his car and the Scottish matron's car would arrive before my Matrix. As luck would have it, they drive off in their late-model Mercedes before my silver chariot appears.

The highlight of my luncheon occurred as I walked out the door. Two of the speaker's associates greeted me by name, and one said, "We'll see you tonight at The Addison." I was thunderstruck. I wondered how they knew my schedule. Had they hacked my computer and found my list of seminars? They informed me that UBS was also a sponsor of the evening seminar. I am confused because I remembered that the invitation was from a Boca Raton office of UBS, not the Palm Beach office, and the names on the invite were completely different. They said that they'd be there for dinner, and the speaker (from J.P. Morgan) would discuss municipal bonds. I informed them that there was no need for me to hear another discussion on the same subject and that I must have made a mistake in signing up for this seminar—and that I wouldn't attend. Their faces fell. They were clearly very disappointed. They literally begged me to attend. They seemed so desperate that I thought about asking if they would pay me to come to dinner, but I didn't. I guessed that they had a poor reception to their mass mailing for tonight's seminar, even worse than the poor response to the luncheon, and that any warm body in a storm would do. I did them a favor and acquiesced.

I returned home at mid-afternoon only to receive some unwelcome news. I always get a second opinion on the treatment for my lymphoma from Dr. Z, the head lymphoma honcho at Sloan Kettering in New York, to whom I was introduced through the courtesy of Errol Cook. The doctor called and recommended I start my next round of chemo now instead of "watching, waiting, and scanning." I had lulled myself into thinking I might be lucky enough to avoid chemo until spring. With this unsettling news on my mind, plus the affects of the caffeine-laced luncheon, I was unable to fall asleep in the afternoon. I typed up some of my notes from the morning seminar, changed my outfit, and as it got darker I headed south for the nightcap.

6:00 p.m. Pull my car up to an almost-empty parking lot in front of The Addison Restaurant and recognize the man from UBS. He is standing by the valet parking sign. Tells me the restaurant is only open for special events (weddings, birthdays, business meetings) and no longer open to the public. That's why there aren't any cars and any valet. He shows me where to park and of course am thrilled to have saved the tip. See him give my car a double take, but he is a consummate gentleman and doesn't ask why a man with $10 million in the market drives a beat-up old car.

Walk with him through the deserted, dimly lit restaurant area to a large private room, in which one table, set for ten, sits forlornly like a wallflower at a high school dance. It was very Felliniesque.

It turns out that the response to UBS's invite is worse than I had anticipated. The only other people who show up are one man and a couple. To add insult to injury, the man is a blowhard (who spends the evening telling us how rich he is and that he doesn't need any investment advice), and the couple are already customers of UBS. (They had come by mistake thinking it was a different seminar run by a competitor.) It becomes a comedy of errors because the seminar that they thought they were going to is the very same one that I had been unceremoniously thrown out of a few nights ago.

7:00 p. m. Salad and filet (medium, thank you) are served. I'd write that the lettuce seems familiar, but you'd think I am paranoid.

Presentation is pretty interesting. Particularly like one of the suits from UBS. Seems quite professional and knowledgeable.

7:30 p.m. The conversation is dragging at the table. Blowhard starts to recount another story about how rich he is and decide can't stomach his braggadocio any longer. Pass up dessert; say thanks and excuse myself. Exit through the deserted restaurant.

In case you are not familiar with The Addison, it is a historic restored mansion by the architect Addison Mizner. The restaurant advertises that they are the only 5-Star Award-Winning restaurant in Boca Raton. I wanted to check it, so I googled the name and then went to "Menu," and lo and behold, this is what comes up.

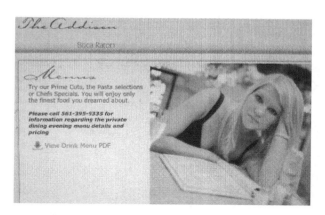

She looks like the best thing on the menu.

I know the picture isn't very clear, but it's clear enough for you to wonder (as I did) what the blonde babe has to do with the 5-Star Award restaurant's menu.

I looked everywhere for her on my visit, but she seemed to have flown the coop. I even checked in the men's room.

WHAT THE HELL AM I DOING HERE?

I have seminar scouts located all over the area—sworn to send me a copy of every free meal invitation they receive. My best scout in the Boynton Beach area is Dr. G, my dermatologist. I didn't think twice when he sent me a fax of an invite from MetLife for a lunch seminar at The Capital Grille, and I called to make a reservation.

When I walked into the private dining room, where I've been so many times that I might even leave a change of clothes there, I faced a rectangular table of sixteen filled with much younger men, all in business attire. (My sweater, short pants, cane, and grey hair stuck out like a sore thumb. I know how that fish out of water must feel.)

12:00 p.m. Slink into chair and try to look yuppie-like. Speaker, a pension lawyer, announces subject, "Fiduciary Protection & Responsibilities for the Business Owner/Plan Sponsor." Well, I don't have a business; don't have a plan; and my only fiduciary responsibility is to my readers to go to as many free lunch seminars as I can and report my findings.

It was a long hour.

Lousy lunch: fried calamari (ugh), hamburger or shrimp (only four) on a bed of grass, or a Caesar salad. Pass on dessert and head out at 1:00 p.m. with my gift, a Snoopy doll, courtesy MetLife.

After a quick visit to my oncological surgeon to check on how my incision was coming along, I headed home, eager for my afternoon nap, only to wind up in the middle of a maelstrom. Judy had invited a couple for dinner at our club and to visit our home afterward for coffee and dessert. Since we were having visitors, Judy decided that the house needed a little work. So when I came home I had to make my way around Jose, who was cleaning the windows and pavers ($80); Sven, who was cleaning the pool (no charge); Melissa, who was cleaning the house ($140); George's gardeners, who put new plantings around the pool ($250); and Larry, who was cleaning the rugs and marble floors ($400). I had never realized I was living in such a pigsty.

It was difficult to find a room in which to take a nap, but the cat and I hid out in our bunker.

When we awoke, the house looked resplendent. I could tell Kitty wished she were having friends over, so she could show off her spick-and-span digs.

Then boom! The phone rang, and I could tell from the ringtone that bad news was forthcoming. Sure enough, our guests for the evening called to cancel—she had the flu. What were we to do with a sparkling clean home and no one to see it? It felt like the story of the tree that falls in the forest. Does it make a sound if no one is there to hear it fall? Was our house really clean if no one could see it?

Our only hope was that we could meet some new friends in the next week or two. Maybe I can pick up a friendly duo at my next free lunch seminar. I hope so—or else it's bye, bye, $870.

THE QUEEN OF STEAK

It's not just another day at the office. I'm off to Ruth's Chris Steak House for my fourth incursion, but I'm waiting to hear from my oncologist as to when my next round of chemo will start. I could call in sick and not go to Ruth's, but I have my readers to consider.

6:00 p.m. Enter private room at Ruth's Chris Steak House. Take a seat in a packed room of forty-six carnivores. Pick up menu. Waiter (Tim) arrives and asks, "Have you ever been to Ruth's Chris before?" He's the very same waiter who asks me the very same question every time I eat here. Answer no so that he has to go into his routine about, "butter on the steaks, steaks on a five-hundred-degree plate, yada, yada, yada."

As a change of pace, order chicken, stuffed with cheese, (lousy choice, find out later). Everyone else in the room orders the six-ounce filet with two shrimp perched on top. Salad and dessert included.

Take out my cell phone to put it on vibrate. Expecting a call from my oncologist. Plan to take the call when it arrives, as I'm anxious to get started. Unbelievably, phone's not working. Lights up, but is frozen. Try everything to get it to work, all to no avail. Decide to remain at seminar and see if there is a message from the doctor at home on my other phone.

6:14 p.m. Pat (head of out-of-state headquartered financial advisory firm) tells us he will finish presentation in one hour. Great news. Topic is "Ten Biggest Mistakes Retirees Make." Expounds his litany of investor's errors, and surprisingly enough, the way to prevent each and every one of these mistakes is to become a client of his firm. Goes so far as to intimate that it's not safe to have your account at Merrill Lynch or Morgan Stanley (et al). He is very careful with his words, but sure wants to plant the seed in the audiences' minds that an investor's securities should not be left there, or they might be "Madoffed." His advice: use a separate custodian firm and a different advisor (him).

Tells about his thorough research of stocks. Cites McDonald's, which plunged a year or so ago when two of their CEOs died within a short time of one another. Man in audience pipes up, "I wonder where they were eating." Pat bought a load of stock at a very low price for his clients and they made a bundle. Sold out at fifty-eight. Man asks why he didn't wait till it got to seventy-nine. Pat tries to cover by saying he'll buy it again, when it's in the fifties or low sixties—as it will be again. Wonder why the man doesn't ask Pat why he doesn't short the stock at seventy-nine.

Extremely bullish on stocks now. Very wary on bonds. Hates annuities. Says his accounts average 3 percent better performance than S&P 500 index, before his 1-percent fee. Doesn't sound so great to me after hearing about how thoroughly he goes about researching and making investments for his client and all the dough they made on Big Mac. Gets great round of applause at end. Guy next to me was very skeptical when he first sat down, but he's going to become a client, maybe many others, based on reception. Pat reminds guests to sign up for a complimentary portfolio review, but adds the offer is only good for sixty days (yeah, sure).

7:25 p.m. Ends speech and asks for questions.

Man asks, "What is the smallest account you'll manage?"

"Yours," Pat replies.

My only question was for Tim (my waiter friend), "Can you box up the rest of my chicken for me?" He brings small black box and stuffs in the stuffed chicken breast. Hope one of my cats will eat it so it doesn't go to waste. Evidently none of the other forty-five guests have cats at home, because mine is the only box in sight.

I hurried out through the almost-deserted restaurant. It was half empty, either due to the lackluster economy or the fact that Pat held this same free dinner seminar on the two previous nights at Ruth's Chris—so that anyone who paid their own tab was a fool.

I rushed home to see if there was a message from my oncologist. He had left word that I should start my coming round of chemo next Monday. I'll be going for treatments for two days in a row every twenty-eight days for about six months. I have no idea how my body is going to tolerate the new drug and whether I'll be able to continue my adventures in restaurant-land. A sobering end to the day, but I've been here before.

NO-FRILLS HERE

Thanksgiving had come and gone. It was one week after my first series of chemo infusions, and I was back in the saddle heading south toward Golden Corral Buffet. I must admit to having been excited, not because I was able to get back to work so soon, but for the opportunity to try out a new restaurant (and one with a western theme, to boot).

I checked out their menu on the Internet: "Golden Corral's legendary, endless dinner buffet features an enormous variety with fifteen proteins, including USDA grilled to order sirloin steaks, pork, seafood, shrimp, and chicken. We are especially proud to serve USDA sirloin." USDA, but what grade, I wondered.

An all-faith cemetery/mausoleum and a sectarian funeral chapel conglomerate sponsored fifteen seminars in November 2010. When I called to make my reservation, I asked how long I'd be at the restaurant. The voice on the other end of the phone told me that the seminar started at 4:30 p.m. and ended at 5:15 p.m. "You can start eating at 5:16 p.m. and eat as quickly or slowly as you like," he continued.

I couldn't wait to dig my teeth into their sirloin steak and compare it to the ones I've been eating at Ruth's, Morton's, et al.

I have a real cowboy hat and boots, which I haven't worn in over thirty years, sitting in my closet waiting for just the right occasion, and if this isn't it, what is? Would Judy let me out of the house looking like Tom Mix? I compromised with myself by settling into a long-sleeved shirt emblazoned with scenes of horses and other western themes and a pair of dirty jeans.

I considered renting a horse for a few hours, but I don't think there is a toll lane for animals on the Florida Turnpike.

4:25 p.m. Arrive at the Corral and hitch my car to a tree. Feel like a bandit on my way to pull off another heist.

4:30 p.m. Herded through restaurant, which has quite a few people already chowing down at the early-bird trough, into back room. This private area would make any Spartan proud—it resembles a cross between a school lunchroom and a prison cafeteria.

Sign in, branded, take seat at a metal table. More than twenty other rather plainly dressed guests positioned around room. I refer to the other guests in this slightly derogatory manner because I'm the only one dressed for the occasion—sporting my western shirt and jeans.

Salesman hunkers down next to me and examines the personal info sheet I had filled out. Asks why I came to a meeting about cemeteries in Margate, which is quite a distance from my home. He's suspicious that I'm a freeloader. Tell him that I'm looking for a cemetery in this area because the Festival Flea Market is nearby, and my wife goes shopping there on a regular basis—and if I'm buried nearby, she can kill two birds with one stone. He looks at me quizzically, decides there is lower fruit to pick and moves on to the next guest.

Everything is on the cheap at this seminar. Besides the $9.95 price tab for the early-bird dinner, there isn't a pad, pencil, or brochure in sight. Wonder if the cemetery plots are cheap, but the speaker doesn't give any prices because he states each deal is custom made.

4:40 p.m. Cemetery spokesperson proclaims he represents largest company in field. Selling "Pre-Planning Packages For Death" to put a family's affairs in order and lock in current price. Declares, "If you could pay $5,000 or $10,000 or $15,000 for a funeral, I'm sure everyone in this room would chose to pay $5,000." All agree except thin-faced woman seated diagonally from me who raises her hands and says, "Ten thousand." Speaker is taken aback, and she sticks to her guns without explaining why. He continues as if she doesn't exist, "No one in my twenty years has ever wanted anything but the cheapest funeral, and that's what we're here to give you and with the best service."

Queries, "Is there any reason not to make pre-arrangements for your funeral?" Another woman answers that you don't need to pre-plan if you're a millionaire and you don't have to worry about money. Speaker asks, "Are there any millionaires in this room?" Room goes silent, except for the incessant Muzak that can't be turned off.

5:05 p. m. Finishes speech early. Salespeople ride in and lasso one prospect at a time. They sit up close and personal with each guest and try to sign him or her up for the inevitable one-on-one. (It brings to mind a scene where cowboys tie up an animal to brand him.) I demur. No problem. Not sure how many others sign up. A few dash out to the buffet. Right behind me.

The restaurant is furnished in early "plain pipe rack." There are steam tables galore, with a variety of dishes that boggle the mind. Head for the USDA grilled sirloin station. Doesn't look like any cut of steak I've ever seen before. (Interestingly enough, there never was a line for steak, as if the regulars were educated consumers.) Take a slice, along with a fried chicken leg, stuffing and sweet potatoes with marshmallows. Pass up the meat loaf, pot roast, Asian dishes, salad, imitation crab salad, freshly baked breads, a tired-looking turkey on the bone, and almost any other food you can think of.

THE ADVENTURES OF A FREE LUNCH JUNKIE

Woman approaches me. Inquires if I came out of the seminar room. She discloses she and her husband have a crypt they'd like to sell and wonders if I would be interested in buying it. All I have on my mind is eating, and she wants me to buy a crypt. Talk about appetite suppressants. She's dejected when I tell her my plate is full right now.

The steak isn't bad. The chicken had been sitting awhile. Then on to a double helping of pineapple topping over chocolate yogurt mixed with peach cobbler and re—topped with juicy candies.

On my way out meet the manager and ask him if the sirloin steaks are USDA. He answers, "Of course they are."

"What grade are they?" I counter.

"Prime!" is his reply.

I'm thunderstruck and wonder if he truly believes it or if that's what he was told to say. Either way he's well on his way to becoming an annuity salesman and giving his own seminars.

PS. I e-mailed Golden Corral and they told me their USDA Grade was "choice." It's possible. At around 5:30 p. m. I was back in my car. I had to hand over $1 in tolls, plus a couple of bucks for the gas, but I came out ahead.

EVERYTHING INCLUDING THE
KITCHEN SINK FOR $10

Before you turnip your nose at the "All You Can Eat For $10"
meal at The Golden Corral take a look at their everyday menu.

Assorted Steamed Vegetable
Awesome Pot Roast
Baked Potatoes
Banana Pudding
Bourbon Street Chicken
Broccoli
Cabbage
Carrot Cake
Carrots
Cauliflower
Chocolate Cake w/ Chocolate Frosting
Clam Chowder
Coleslaw
Corn
Fresh fruit
Fried Chicken
Fudgy Brownies
Green Beans
Greens

Grilled-to-order USDA Sirloin Steaks (*dinner only)
Macaroni & Cheese
Macaroni Salad
Mashed Potatoes & Gravy
Meatloaf
No Sugar Added Chocolate Pudding
Pizza
Potato Salad
Rotisserie Chicken
Seafood Salad
Soft Serve Ice Cream
Spaghetti
Sugar Free Red Gelatin
Sweet Potatoes
Timberline Chili
Yeast Rolls
50+ Toppings on our Fresh Cold Salad Bar

CAN I PULL IT OFF?

December 2, 2010, would mark our forty-fifth wedding anniversary. I've been going out to dine, day after day, to all of the area's finest restaurants in my research for this book, so it would be no big deal for me to go mega-restaurant to celebrate, but of course Judy has stayed at home, knitting, while I've been at work, and she wanted to celebrate in style, befitting the momentous occasion. Wow, that was a mouthful.

Here's my dilemma. Suppose I get an invitation for a free dinner seminar at, say, Morton's or Ruth's for December 2? I'd hate to pass it up, and I could kill another two birds with one stone. Guests are welcome, so I could easily sign us both up. Judy'd be thrilled to go to Morton's for the celebration, but how could I explain to her who all the other people are who are sitting at our table, and why she has to wear a name tag in a restaurant, and what is that man doing talking about annuities while we're eating a great meal. Quite a conundrum.

Fortunately for me the problem never came up, as no invites came in for December 2. Since it's our forty-fifth, I decided to splurge and made a reservation at Three Forks, a relative newcomer on the Boca scene, but I'd heard a few good comments, and the Web site showcased a beautiful dining room.

We had a great meal, and it turned out to be a freebie. Judy treated me. I guess she felt incredibly indebted since I bought her a Sonicare Toothbrush to celebrate the momentous occasion.

When we got home our son, Bill, called to congratulate us. We learned it was only our forty-fourth anniversary. What am I going to give Judy next year to top the Sonicare? Maybe a set of refill brushes?

SIX FREEBIES IN THREE
DAYS—WHAT RECESSION?

These were the days that tested my commitment to my readers. Two steak houses, one fine Chinese restaurant, one Cheesecake Factory, and pancake breakfasts at two assisted living facilities—all within fifty-six hours. I know how Ike must have felt on the morning of June 4, 1944.

And besides the rigors of my schedule, I had to weather a severe cold snap in South Florida, with morning temperatures only a frigid handful of degrees over freezing forecast for the entire period. But I realize there's no one else to do this noble work, so I pulled my car up to Ruth's Chris at a little before noon to start on my marathon-eating/listening/writing orgy. (Unfortunately, at my age the old-fashioned orgies are beyond my reach.)

I don't even want to burden you with the frustrations of that Monday morning, when at 9:05 a.m. I called to make sure that the first seminar was still being held and was told that my name wasn't on the list and there wasn't room for anyone else. I pulled a John Boehner, and somehow they found room for me, saying, "They're going to squeeze one seat in, but you'll have to sit at a diagonal to the table." I guessed I'd just have to be careful to avoid my neighbor's knife as he dug into his filet.

This was my fifth visit to Ruth's and my forty-first seminar in seven months.

12:00 p.m. Arrive at Ruth's. Too cold to park in nearby free lot, so have to leave car with valet. Young man takes car and gives me a ticket and a look. Wonder if he recognizes me and remembers I'm a dollar tipper. Maybe it's just my paranoia. Get in line to register. Name tagged. Enter familiar private room, which is mostly filled. Unfortunately recognize two people we've known for many years. There is a free seat next to them, so there is no way to avoid joining their table. Say unfortunately, not because don't like them, but because I won't be able to interview other attendees for this write-up. Norma and Al are salt of the earth Midwesterners who are wealthy and very philanthropic. If they knew I was here to grub a free meal, they'd be horrified. And to make matters worse they are life insurance clients of the sponsor and were asked to come to the luncheon to give a testimonial. (Forget to ask them if they are attending all five seminars the host is giving.) Interestingly enough they met the sponsor at a free lunch seminar years ago.

12:05 p.m. Tim is my waiter for the fourth time. Asks me, "Have you ever been to Ruth's Chris before?" I'm embarrassed in front of my friends and the other three guests at the table to answer no, but do so to punish him for not recognizing me. He has to go into his thirty-second prerecorded speech about five-hundred-degree plates and butter on all steaks, etc. I think I see Al nudge Norma when I say haven't been to Ruth's before. (Later on I'm sure he nudged her, because out of nowhere he asks me, "Did you lose a lot of money in the stock market's decline?")

12:10 p.m. Stuart calls the meeting to order. Starts off by calling on Norma to give her testimonial, which she does with effusive gusto. She doesn't need the five free meals, so I believe in her sincerity. However, our host omits one important fact. He doesn't tell us Norma and Al are only life insurance clients—they use another firm to manage their

sizeable investments—and since most of Stuart's pitch has to do sell-
ing annuities, he's misleading the other thirty-two guests in the room.
But he's an annuity salesman and for many of the ones I've met that's
par for the course And judging by the audience this is a par three
course.

12:15 p.m. Salad is served. Stuart's son takes over mike. His thrust
is that all types of investments are lousy and only place to put your
money is in annuities. Asserts CDs have terrible yield and intimates
that FDIC insurance is suspect. Stocks stink. "Do you have enough time
left in your life to recover from the next major stock market decline?"
appears in bold letters on the screen. "Don't buy gold—no intrinsic
value and muni's are not safe."

He paraphrases famous Harvard professor's lecture of two weeks
ago, proclaiming that the stock market will have a steep decline within
two years. Room shudders.

His "Fixed Indexed Annuities" are the only place to put your
money—they yield 2–7 percent, and your money is safe.

12:35 p.m. My filet arrives. Perfectly cooked and delicious. Feel ter-
rible biting the hand that feeds me by having made negative com-
ments about the father and son's presentation, but soon get over it.
Al burns his hand on the five-hundred-degree plate. Maybe he's never
been here before.

Woman at table says she sold out all her stocks during the stock
market's decline and has been sitting in cash ever since. The market's
roared back (doubling since the low), and she's in money market funds,
making less than 1 percent. She's afraid to get back in to the market, as
are the millions of Americans who sold out and have their money on the
sidelines. They are sure that the day they put their money back in the
market, it will dive again—and who can blame them, it probably will.

1:25 p.m. Gustatory note: Thirty-three of the guests order the filet;
one orders crab cakes, and two opt for chicken. Four people pick their

teeth with their fingers and three people ask for doggie bags. Not sure if the doggie-baggers are the teeth pickers. Next time I'll pay better attention. Dessert is overly sweet cheesecake. Hope to do better tonight at The Cheesecake Factory.

Stuart closes with five minutes on life insurance and then five more on estate planning. Says next year estate tax going way up from zero to 55 percent. Woman comes out with, "I should die this year." Stuart replies, "Eat your dessert first."

Woman who told us she's sitting all in cash tells Al she really liked the presentation. Bye, bye, cash—annuities are on the way.

1:40 p.m. Not a toothpick in sight. Pick my teeth with fingers and get up to leave.

On the way home I passed several previously vacant lots adorned with forests of Christmas trees. Many are spruced up with lights. Yes, Virginia, there is a Christmas (tree) in Boca. To get into the spirit of the season, I tuned in a FM station that broadcasts Xmas music 24/7. A smile came to my face as I listened to Bing crooning, "White Christmas."

I fell into bed exhausted, as I didn't have time for my morning nap. I got up at three, wrote this segment till five, dressed, freshened up, and then got back in my car for my 6 o'clock appointment at The Cheesecake Factory. Maybe on this, my second seminar visit, they'll serve fried chicken and mashed with gravy.

LET THEM EAT BREAD!

Marie Antoinette had nothing on Mr. X of a major insurance conglomerate. I sat in my chair at a table at his dinner seminar from 6:00 p.m. to 7:45 p.m. without a scrap of food to eat (except some bread) while three different speakers talked endlessly about estate planning, can't-miss annuities, life insurance and long-term health care.

And to add insult to injury there wasn't any salad course, and of course there wasn't any dessert course, and of course part of my chicken piccata was uncooked. I'd like to do to Mr. X what they did to poor old Marie A.

Please excuse my acerbic vitriol, but I like to eat at a reasonable hour (6:00 p.m.) like any fun-loving senior. And if I'm invited to The Cheesecake Factory for dinner, I expect to eat cheesecake—or else Mr. X should have invited me to the No Salad /No Cheesecake Factory.

Well, enough of my recriminations, here's my blow-by-blow description of what transpired between 6 p.m. and 8:15 p.m. at this seminar.

6:00 p.m. Enter private room and see four men in suits and no guests in a room with six tables of four. Bad omen. They sign me in

and say the cold weather must have delayed the others. Go to men's room to kill time and take a picture. Return to empty room and chat with salespeople. Tell me they give one of these seminars each month at this restaurant and usually get a good turnout. Use mailing lists and get a response of close to 1 percent but of these only two thirds show up. Figure if they sell one annuity every year, they come out way ahead.

6:30 p.m. Four couples and one single straggle in. Each sit at a separate table. Salesman goes to each new arrival's table and makes nice. No one comes to my table. Never thought I'd meet an annuity salesman who was fussy about a potential client's personal hygiene.

Terrence (a lawyer in a sweater and no tie) makes an excellent presentation about wills and estate planning. Many questions. Learn something that may be important. He has a terrible cold, so never approach him, but may call to follow up.

7:15 p.m. Professional speaker pitches variable annuities. No sign of dinner. Stomach not interested in annuities. Too hungry to take any notes.

7:45 p. m. New speaker promises food is on its way. I had chosen chicken over Steak Diane because when I was single, a gal named Diane gave me a hard time. (Come to think of it, if I cut out all foods that had a gal's name who had given me a hard time, I'd be a lot thinner.) Spit out uncooked piece of chicken. Enough's enough. Head for exit.

I passed a display case bulging with a panoply of cheesecakes, which seemed to mock me. They were priced at $6.95 per delicious chunk. I passed. Hoped I don't get salmonella. Hoped Mr. X does.

Say, "Cheese."

THIS IS A CLASSIC

The heading above is not a characterization of today's story about my luncheon seminar at a nearby Independent Living Facility (ILF). It's just that the *name* of the ILF I visited is Classic Residence. The 154-room community is part of a nationwide chain owned by the Pritzker family of Chicago.

"Thar's money in them there ills," one Pritzker is rumored to have said as his reason for building this conglomerate to cash in on America's aging population's need for pre-hospice housing.

I arrived promptly at eleven o'clock, eager to taste the "savory cuisine" touted in the mailed invitation. And I know I'm jumping the gun, but the food was delicious. Now let's get down to the nitty-gritty.

11:05 Sign in, get a tag, and led to meeting room. Coffee, fruit, and cheese available. Janet motions me to join her table. She's a resident who volunteers to meet and greet prospective residents. Shake hands with Beatriz and her sister, who are here to scout out the place for their older brother. All three women at the table are widows.

Beatriz is originally from Columbia. Still accented. Likes to keep active going to museums, theater, etc., in Palm Beach area where she lives. She seems like a kindred soul, so lean over and whisper to her that

I'm at the meeting because am writing a book about free lunch semi-nars. She smiles. Janet doesn't smile. She says reproachfully, "I heard what you said," and raises her hand to summon one of the adminis-trators. I continue talking to Beatriz in a louder voice and say, "My wife and I will likely consider moving to an assisted facility in a few years." At that moment Beatriz's sister happens to ask Janet a question and distracts her. Hold my breath. At that moment the sales presentation begins, and it appears I've dodged the bullet. But worry that Janet's gun has another slug in it with my name (Earl) on it.

Short slide show tells about the Pritzker's nineteen communities in eleven states. Answers questions about dogs ("We love them as long as they are under twenty-five pounds"); leases ("One year with annual increases of about 3 percent; our competitors who offer three-year leases have to skimp on service"); and tenants who run out of money ("We put you out; there's no better way to put it").

12:00 p.m. In we troop to lunch. Careful not to sit with my back to Janet. Join a resident, an employee, and a couple from Baltimore. Lovely room, just right for the fifty or so guests. Put napkin in lap and take a good hard look at the dish in front of me. It looks like tuna with something green shredded on top. Tablemates also in quandary. Finally chef walks by, and we learn it's crabmeat topped with sea-weed. Can you imagine my first encounter with seaweed on a plate is in a retirement community in Boca Raton? I throw the seaweed back in the ocean and enjoy my crab unadorned. Baltimore man says only good crab is from his home state.

All three women at the table are or were once widowed. The fifty-ish gal, who works for Classic Residence in sales, tells how hard it is being single in a couple's world. She lost all her old friends and moved to Florida to try to start over. So far, still alone. Married woman guest echoes these comments. She's furious with the predatory widows she's had to come up against who even prey upon married men.

Very tasty salad. Tenderloin of beef is delicious. The two grilled shrimp are a bit of overkill. Surf and turf are like oil and water to me.

Baltimore man says they had a <u>free</u> three-night, four-day stay at The Forum, an assisted living facility nearby. How did I ever miss out on that? Casts a pall over the whole day.

I'm very tired, after being deprived of my morning nap, and then having all the tension about Janet almost blowing my cover. I bid good-bye to my tablemates and passed up the homemade chocolate lava cake. You are not allowed to take food out via doggie bag at any assisted community I've visited so far.

My compliments to the chef. The meal was a classic.

KNEE HOW, MORGAN STANLEY*

The evening festivities got off to an inauspicious start when I pulled up to the gatehouse at Broken Sound to pick up Herb on the way to our dinner seminar. The guard asked me whom I was visiting. I could not, for the life of me, remember Herb's last name. I've only known him for twenty years. I plaintively asked the guard if he knew a family whose first names were Herb and Marlene. He gave me that look. The car behind me started to honk. The guard was just about to tell me to pull over when their name popped into my head. He pushed a button to raise the barrier in front of my car, and I pulled away. I looked out the rearview mirror and saw him shake his head.

The bad taste from this incident soon disappeared from my mouth because we were headed for Uncle Tai's, an excellent Chinese restaurant. We parked in the free lot and walked to Boca Center, which is adorned with glistening Christmas lights and a large menorah. The management company played it safe as far as seasonal decorations are concerned. It's cold enough outside to feel like a New York December.

* *Knee how* does not mean "how to give a knee to" Morgan Stanley. It's Chinese for hello.

6:00 p.m. Led to private back room. Long table set for about six-teen. Greeted. No nametags. Sure sign of a classy operation. Janus (a large mutual fund) is the sponsor and Morgan Stanley hosts it. Menu is copied on three-by-five piece of paper. Wonton or egg roll; choice of four ordinary entrees; no dessert. Take back what I said about a classy operation.

Neighbors on our left introduce themselves. Single couple. Man is pretty showy. Brings a date, who is Asian. Wonder if he rented her to make an impression.

Married couple on our right are pleasant, almost as old as I am. We play Jewish geography. (Whenever Jews meet, they exchange info about where they were born, lived, etc., and soon find they are first cousins.) He (Al) and I were both Brooklyn born and CPAs. His wife's first husband lived in the same building I once did in Manhattan. We hug; we're mishpocha (Yiddish for family).

They are clients of Morgan Stanley and very happy with the gal who handles their account. She's the one running this event. He's also quite defensive about his advisers—because when happen to men-tion that the guest speaker from Janus didn't say a thing, he gets a bit snippy.

A couple from my community sit next to them. They were also at a free seminar dinner I attended a few weeks ago. They didn't recognize me then and they don't recognize me now, even though I pass him in the Bagel Breakfast Room before tennis three days a week. Another proof that I'm so forgettable.

Way down the table someone mentions "Madoff." The wife's head jerks around. They were unfortunate victims.

6:15 p.m. Ginger welcomes everyone. Thanks us for coming. (I take it personally.) Asks do we know the difference between try and triumph. No one guesses. It's "umph," and she and Morgan Stanley are here to supply it to our portfolios. Says expression comes from seventeenth-century Marquessa (who I assume spoke English when she wanted to be quoted at a Chinese restaurant).

Meal is served during speeches. Egg roll. Chicken dish, no big deal. Herb looks at his plate and can't remember what he ordered. Eats it. Likes it. Has no idea what it is.

Al's wife picks a peck of peppers from her dish, places them in a cup, doesn't eat the chicken, and then asks for a doggie bag. Nudge her husband, who just shrugs his shoulders.

Janus has prepared an expensive brochure titled, "Preparing For Higher Taxes"—only trouble is this afternoon Obama announced he favors two-year extension of Bush tax cuts. Bye, bye, brochure. (Maybe bye, bye, Barack.)

7:45 p.m. Dzai Jyan (bye, bye in Mandarin), Morgan Stanley.

Herb and I agreed a good time was had by all, but that Ginger could have put a little more "umph" in the menu. Uncle Tai serves a crispy whole fish, Hunan style, that is to die for, but who am I to carp?

HERE'S ANOTHER SING-ALONG

Judy: "Baby, it's cold outside."
Earl: "I really can't stay."
Judy: "But baby, it's cold outside."
Earl: "I've got to go away."

If you were in my home at eight thirty on the morning of December 8 (with the temperature outside a frigid, for South Florida, forty-seven degrees), these were the words you would have heard as Judy tried to dissuade me from leaving for my 9 a.m. pancake breakfast seminar, which was a cold thirty-minute drive away at a retirement home. I showed my wife the mailer/invitation, which featured a tantalizing photo of a heaping plate of steaming hot Aunt Jemima's finest pancakes smothered with Florida farm-fresh butter and Vermont maple syrup, all topped with four pieces of hickory-smoked, crisp Virginia bacon.

Judy implored, "I'll make you pancakes and bacon, and you won't have to go out in this cold."

"No, thanks," I replied, "I owe it to my readers to personally check out The Aston Gardens Community at Parkland and see if it lives up to its award-winning title."

Thirty minutes later I pulled into the parking lot, eagerly awaiting the first bite of my pancakes and bacon. They better be "as advertised," because I will have invested $2.50 in tolls and $15 in gas by the time I've made the round trip.

9:05 a.m. Sign in, name tagged, and directed to dining room. Sure enough, there's a row of steam tables with pancakes, bacon, syrup, bagels, eggs, fruit, juice, and coffee. Fill my plate and sit at an almost-empty table. Greeted by friendly resident (Gloria), who is assigned to this table. Tries to engage me in conversation while I'm only interested in eating breakfast. Dig in anyway. "How was it?" you ask. "Nothing special—some of the pancakes were a bit undercooked and not hot off the griddle," I reply. But that verdict didn't stop me from taking seconds on the flapjacks and adding a half a bagel with eggs and bacon. "Free" always makes food taste better.

Joined by Gene, a guest whose wife is in a nursing home. He lives in Century Village and asks if Aston Gardens takes people via Medicaid. He gets the expected turndown from the director of community development (Rebecca), who has joined us. Her tight-fitting white slacks show off her sleek figure to advantage—and not too shabby a face. Without further ado, rate this the best retirement community in South Florida.

"Miss Retirement Community" next turns her attention to me as a potential prospect. Asks where I live. Embarassed to tell her that I live in a gated community, so name a rental complex. She brightens up and says they have several residents from that area. In our conversation she relates that they have several important people staying at Aston Gardens. Name-drops Jean Nidetch, founder of Weight Watchers. Turn to Gloria and ask her if Nidetch has stayed slim in her golden years. She answers, "You know as we grow old, everything that was north goes south."

Gene (the man whose wife is in a nursing home) flirtatiously remarks to Gloria that she's too young to be living in a retirement home. She retorts laughingly, "Words like that will get you everything."

This innocent banter continues during breakfast. Gene is a short, bedraggled-looking, impoverished, almost pitiful remnant of a man, probably with a high school equivalency diploma—but with a kind disposition and a crooked smile. The widow Gloria is a plain, but pleasant-enough-looking, ex-math schoolteacher from Long Island. Gene's attention makes her morning, and he seems to be enjoying the social intercourse.

Gloria recounts a story from her later days in Rhinebeck, New York, about Chelsea Clinton's wedding there. Many of the town's residents were inconvenienced during the weekend celebrations by the traffic dislocation caused by the influx of guests, press, and sightseers. Bill and Hillary sent a bottle of vintage wine to forty of the homeowners in the neighborhood as a peace offering (wonder why he didn't include a fine Cuban cigar to enjoy with the libation).

9:40 a.m. Short video about the community shown to the fifty-plus guests followed by a Q&A. Speaker asks anyone who wants to take a tour of the facilities to raise their hands. Only a handful raise their hands. Must be a bunch of lousy freeloaders in attendance. Gene, after all that flirting with Gloria, leaves without even saying good-bye to her. Ruins her day.

In the hallway the residents have created a wall of photos, all taken when they were young. It's quite a shock to view all these youthful faces and vibrant bodies and compare them to the seniors moving haltingly past. The scene reminds me of a sculptural installation I created when I was an artist. I built a wall piece consisting of a bathroom sink with a mirrored medicine cabinet above it. As a viewer looked in the mirror, these words appeared: "I wonder what happened to the face of the young man who used to look out at me."

As I'm leaving encounter a pair of attendees discussing their reaction to Aston Gardens. One of them favorably compares it to another facility they had visited by commenting, "This is more hamish" (Yiddish for homelike). I think Aston Gardens should put this testimonial on its mailers and brochures instead of the picture of the pancakes.

Visiting all these facilities has been an emotional strain. "There, but for the grace of God, go I."

And perhaps someday in the future, "There, with the grace of my John Hancock Long-Term Health-Care Policy, I'll be there."

I wondered if Miss Retirement Community of 2010 will still be there. (Just kidding, Judy.)

BACK AT THE SCENE OF THE CRIME

or

BABY IT'S COLD OUTSIDE,
BENJY, THERE'S A BABY INSIDE

or

I'M FORGETTABLE, THAT'S WHAT I AM

or

IS CHICKEN A MIS-STEAK AT MORTON'S?

or

WHO EATS CHEESECAKE WITH HIS FINGERS?

I couldn't figure out which of the above titles was the most appropriate to headline this story about Wednesday evening's dinner seminar, my sixth adventure in a hectic three-day period, so I decided to use them all.

As I pulled up to Morton's Steakhouse, it was so cold outside that I take pity on the young valet parker shivering in his thin parka and left my car with him to park. I noticed another steak-restaurant-bound couple leave their car in the free parking lot and walk to dinner. Cheapskates.

Morton's is just a stone's throw from Uncle Tai's, the scene of last night's seminar. (This is the same stone I used to kill two birds with—one of which I ate for dinner, but I'm getting ahead of myself.)

6:30 p.m. First one to enter private dining room. Greeted by four of them (from Morgan Stanley and Goldman Sachs). Told to take my place card. Scan names of other guests. See name of the Madoff-victimized couple from my community whom I sat only a boulder's throw away from last night at Ruth's Chris. Tell Suzy (one of the Morgan Stanly contingent) I recognize one couple's name. She asks if want to have them seated with me. Say no. She smiles.

Sit next to pleasant couple from Boston—ex-coat manufacturer. We exchange small talk. Ask wife if they have been to other seminars. When she answers in the affirmative, I inquire if she ever found any interesting. She replies, "Yes, but I can't think of why."

Five tables fill up rapidly. Couple I'm avoiding come in, and sure enough, sits down at table facing me. He looks me in eye without any recognition. We introduce each other by first names. Boston man asks them where they live. They reply. Boston man says, "That's where Earl lives." They look at me in disbelief. Exchange last names. Wife says, "Judy's husband?" I nod. During the evening they seem interested in tax-free bonds, so happily Madoff didn't get it all.

6:45 p.m. George doffs jacket and welcomes group. As he's talking, a young woman enters with her husband—nothing unusual about that, you say—well, she's carrying a crying infant in her arms. They sit unconcernedly at another table.

George continues his speech, trying not to notice the eight-hundred-pound gorilla in the room. Gives ten specific stock and bond recommendations, unlike many other plain-vanilla (protect your ass) seminar hosts. Hard to hear him over the baby's cries. Baby doesn't seem to mind George talking while he's crying, and neither do his parents.

Feel sorry for George. He's evidently put a lot of time and effort into creating this sales presentation. One male guest adds to the distraction by trying to engage the infant in conversation by making "goo-goo" sounds.

Wonder if I were giving this seminar if I'd ask one of my associates to request the mother to please take the child out of the room. At one point, mother and child leave the room. We all breathe a sigh of relief, only to have her return with a car seat, which she places on the floor. They settle in for the evening. The parents are completely unconcerned about the disturbance the baby is causing. She appears Swedish-American, he Ghanan-American.

6:55 p.m. Wine flows like water. Order tomato juice. Waitress comes back and tells me they are all out of it. Order cranberry. Menu offers four choices for entrée. I'm steaked out and choose chicken, but just about everyone else in the room orders the filet. Salad comes first. Pick New York cheesecake as my dessert choice. Couple with baby order vegetable plate as main course. Think she might breastfeed child during presentation, but guess baby isn't hungry.

Suzy finally steps into the breach and asks if she can pick up the baby and walk it around. (Can't determine if her actions are prompted by a word from her boss.) Takes kid outside, and room's quiet is restored. Walks him for quite awhile. Maybe she takes the baby to Uncle Tai's to spoil their dinners.

7:25 p.m. George says Morgan Stanley expects market to be up 10 percent in 2011. Reports Goldman Sachs predicts 20 percent gain. Program says dinner is sponsored (paid for) by Goldman

Sachs—maybe to atone for selling toxic subprime mortgage deals to customers while the firm was shorting them. Man from Goldman never gets up to say a word. Probably too busy trying to figure out what to spend his bonus on. (There's no onus in a big bonus.)

Suzy gives out contest sheet for all guests. Make your pick as to where the stock averages will be at the end of 2011, and the winner(s) will get a free meal at Morton's. I pick up 5 percent. Baby guesses +10 percent. Same sheet has room to answer yea or nay to request a free consultation with George.

7:50 p.m. Getting tired, but dessert is nowhere to be seen. Ask waiter to box up my uneaten chicken slabs and add my cheesecake. It's a deal. I'm out of there.

I tipped the valet lavishly (by my standards) and point the car north. As I'm drove, I could smell the sweet cream in the New York cheesecake, which was sitting invitingly in a plastic container in the doggie bag on the passenger's seat. I figured if other people could text while driving, I could eat my cake with one hand on the wheel. I dipped my fingers into the generous slice. One good dip deserved four others. My fingers were all gooey, but what a great way to end the evening. I wiped my cheese-covered hand on my pants.

I bet I fell asleep before the baby did.

ROAST PORK AND BLINTZES

I didn't see Mommy kissing Santa Claus at the holiday brunch I attended at Newport Place (a retirement community), but I did see a US Marine eating a blintz. Let me explain.

The community at Boynton Beach invited me to join them for brunch on December 10. But there was a catch. I had to bring an unwrapped gift as part of their benefit for the Marines' Toys For Tots Foundation. The toy had to be valued at no less than $5. I wondered if I would lose my professional standing if I paid for lunch.

I realized it would be hard to make a profit on this deal, considering the gas I'd need for the thirty-five-mile roundtrip. "Bah, humbug," I said to myself, "I'm not in this business to lose money." But I remembered Dickens's description of old Ebenezer: "The cold within him froze his old features, nipped his pointed nose, made his eyes red, his thin lips blue." I decided to splurge, just this once.

I asked Judy to buy a toy and told her she only had to spend $5. You guessed it. She came back with some sort of bear/doll, which was sporting a $9.95 price tag. I scolded her, explaining for that kind of money she could have gotten two toys, and I could have had a free meal next year as well. She said I had red eyes and thin blue lips, so I let the matter rest.

11:00 a.m. Arrive, take elevator to second floor, walk to dining room. Greeted by very pregnant young woman. (Wonder why seminars so often have a pregnant hostess/greeter. Come to no conclusion. Their problem, not mine.) Two Marines stand straight and tall beside a box rapidly filling up with toys. Ask to have my picture taken with them. Ask one of the Marines to sign an IRS Tax Form 8283 verifying that I gave a non-cash charitable contribution of $10.

Toys For Tots.

Long line in dining room for holiday brunch buffet. Everything from pork chops to blintzes and lox to sushi. I surmise they have a diversified resident mix—Christian and Jewish plus a sprinkling of Japanese. (This astute observation is born out later when I spy a giant Christmas tree, a menorah, and a sword in the lobby.)

Fill my plate with selection of food that gives away my religious affiliation. Take a seat at a table with Irving, Arlene, and Marvin. They are eating the same food I am, so feel at home.

Marvin is blind, from Brooklyn, and his wife is back in their apartment, having gotten violently ill during the night. We make small talk, and I stupidly say that thought the grounds were lovely. He passes over my faux pas. Says they've been here a year and a half. Likes it very much, but confides food is only "decent." Today's luncheon is many cuts above decent. I'm only sorry that I had made pancakes out of a spray can, for breakfast only a few hours ago. But mine weren't even decent. Don't know why the bottom of the pancake always gets burnt.

Marines get in buffet line. Pause over steam table with blintzes resting snugly in warmer. They look puzzled (the Marines, not the blintzes). African-American server explains, "They're blintzes. They're good." Figuring they must be better than K rations, they each take one.

i'm overfed and over-assisted livinged, so I beat it out of there. On the way out, I passed a huge Xmas tree. Marvin had told me that next week the community buses in a group of poor children. The residents provide toys, which are placed under the tree for the kids. Sounded like a wonderful experience for all.

One of the residents had set up a table in lobby to sell her daughter's jewelry. I was tempted to buy something for Judy, but it's too soon after her Sonicare toothbrush anniversary gift and too close to her Xmas gift of Sonicare brush refills. Maybe next year.

HOW TO CAPITALIZE ON
SOMEONE ELSE'S DEMISE

As soon as I walked into Ruth's Chris Steak House, I knew I had made a boo-boo. There was the smiling face of the man who had made a presentation at his seminar at Seasons 52 a little over two months ago. I promised myself not to double dip (go back a second time), and here was John extending his hand in welcome. Since the room wasn't nearly full, I decided to stay and try to enjoy my filet, no matter what my readers might think. Compared to what happened at Abu Ghraib, it's not so bad.

11:05 p.m. Sit at one of the six tables with place settings for six. Joined by two couples who came together. Tim (the same waiter I've had on my previous four visits) welcomes us and asks if we have ever been to Ruth's before. They say yes. I say no. He looks me right in the eye and tells me about their 1,800-degree oven, butter and salt on every steak, etc. Felt like saying, "Hey, it's me, Tim. I was here on December 6, November 18, September 21, and July 21." Instead pretend to listen intently to his pre-recorded recitation and then order my filet medium, no butter. Tried to make my face look distinctive, as I looked him right in the eye, maybe he'll recognize me next time.

Ask the couple next to me if they go to seminars frequently. He answers, "Depends on what you mean by frequently." His wife chimes in and tells a story of their last seminar at Morton's, when her husband asked for a cup of coffee. They were told the restaurant doesn't serve coffee till dinner. Her husband went outside to Dunkin' Donuts and brought back a container of java. I can tell he is my kind of guy. This is reinforced when I learn he is a CPA. Later on they admit that they are professional freeloaders. He recounts being turned down once for a seminar because he had been to a previous luncheon. He was surprised they kept records.

John (mine host) spends most of the next two hours talking about life settlements (a financial transaction in which the owner of a life insurance policy sells his policy to a third party). John's pitching (as a broker) a public company named Life Partners, Inc., which offers to its customers a fractional interest in the life insurance policies it purchases. He says investor has to double his money, guaranteed; the only question is how long it takes to get the money back. Life Partners says over past ten years, average return has been in excess of 10 percent. John says usually get money back in two to four years and make big double-digit return! If it takes ten years to get money back, investors make 5 percent annual return. So you're praying for the people whose policies you bought a piece of to die quickly (nothing personal, and you don't get to know the name of the person whose policy you own a piece of, for obvious reasons).

John says major Wall Street firms are the primary investors in these policies. "If you're a client of Merrill Lynch, they won't tell you about these investments," speaker intones. "They keep them for themselves." I'm furious he so spurious.

Despite the promise of high returns on their investment, many of the people at the luncheon are offended by the whole concept, i.e., betting on when someone will die and rooting for his or her early expiration (especially on an empty stomach—ours, not the deceased's). Several dark jokes are passed around: "Do I have to attend the funeral?" "Is it proper to send flowers?" "Can I visit them in the hospital?"

In order to qualify to be able to buy these fractional interests, investor must have a net worth of at least $1 million or annual income of $200,000. Most of the people in our room appear not to be in that category, but if John reels in one person, he's paid for the luncheon.

12:30 p.m. Guests getting hungry and not interested in hearing anything further about life settlements, or anything else, for that matter. John's assistant opens door to our room to stealthily signal that the salad course is sitting outside. She's signaled to cool it. Guests keep getting up to go to the john. They pass the salads wilting in the passageway. John is oblivious. He enjoys talking and has a captive audience. Seems like a nice, happy-go-lucky guy. Often laughs inappropriately. Says Ed McMahon was broke and sold his policy for $1 million to Life Partners. Can you imagine how prestigious it would be to own a piece of a celebrity's policy? (Be the only one in your community to own a piece of Ed McMahon.) Asserts so many people waiting to buy fractional interests in policies that you have to wait ninety days.

1:15 p.m. John innocently asks, "Do they have the food ready yet?" We all answer. "Yes! Mutiny avoided. Salad, steak, and dessert follow in quick order. A good time is had by all.

I exited and gave my ticket to the valet. When I entered the car, I could not find my sunglasses. I always leave them in the same spot. I searched the car; I searched the attendant; I can't find them.

The attendant went through the car and found my glasses in the glove compartment. I had never before in all my life put my glasses in the glove compartment. But this time when I left the car with the valet, I was looking for a paper in the glove compartment and must have put them in by mistake. As I got ready to pull away, the attendant pointed the way to the nearest Alzheimer's clinic.

SARTORIAL NOTE: One man came dressed for the occasion in jeans, sneakers, shirt, sweater, and a baseball cap, which he wore backwards all during lunch. There's always someone who makes me look good at these seminars.

SEC NOTE: In January 2011, the SEC announced it is investigating some of the practices of Life Partners. Who knows, maybe the head of the SEC wants to get in on the action.

SPECIAL THANKS:

I've got some room left on the bottom of this page, so I'd like to use it to pay tribute to some of my "scouts' who received many of the invitations to the free lunch seminars and provided them to me.

First is Sandy Kofsky, a dark-haired, tennis-playing beauty.

Second is Paul Shafran, a dark-haired tennis-playing buddy, who has never read a page of my book, and probably never will, because he says it's too dark at the Indian Casino's poker table to be able to read.

Third is Dr. Joseph Gretzula, my dermatologist and fellow contemporary art lover.

A BUSMAN'S HOLIDAY

What does a free lunch junkie do on his night off? He goes to a free dinner seminar, where the topic is, "Updates on Lymphoma Treatment Options." It was held at Gilda's Club in Ft. Lauderdale. Gene Wilder was one of the founders of this organization that offers support to people who have cancer and to their families. The club was named after his wife, comedienne Gilda Radner, who once said, "Cancer gave me membership to an elite club I'd rather not belong to."

It is very difficult for me to convey the emotions I experienced as I sat with a group of forty like-afflicted people who were all here seeking hope and help. We don't look too different on the surface from the groups I've sat with at financial seminars at Ruth's and Morton's. Some of us are fairly young. I'm probably the oldest (but undoubtedly the best looking). But there's death in the air, much like the feeling I've had when I'm in a room in a hospital getting chemo and look around at the many others who are hooked up to their lifelines.

I ate my roast beef sandwich, pickle, potato salad, and gingerbread cookie quickly. I was only interested in whether I might learn something about my cancer that would reassure me about my chances to be able to enjoy many more free lunch seminars. The presentation was detailed and very technical, but there wasn't any good news or bad news, as far as I was concerned.

As the oncologist talked about rates of remission, the fingers on my right hand unconsciously moved to measure the size of the tumor under my left arm—to assess if it was smaller or larger than it had been three hours ago.

When the doctor discussed various clinical trials that were available for lymphoma, my mind raced back to 2005. A new vaccine, Favid, was undergoing clinical trials, and my oncologist recommended that I participate. First, I had a few chemo sessions, and then I started a regimen of four monthly injections—three of which Judy administered at home. Every three months I had a full body CAT scan, which required my drinking thirty ounces of "barium gook."

A year later my tumors had not decreased in size and the treatments were stopped. I was then informed that I had been getting a placebo and that if I wanted, I could get the real thing. So it started all over again—the injections, the chemo, the "gook," and the scans.

I felt buoyed when I learned that the company that manufactured the vaccine had raised $12 million to construct a plant to produce Favid. I was convinced they wouldn't have done this unless they were pretty darn sure that the FDA would approve their trials. As you have undoubtedly guessed, one year later my tumors had grown, the trial was suspended, and the company went belly up. I felt like a black-sheeped guinea pig. This was in the days when I was an artist, and I created this sculpture to memorialize my two years as a stuck pig.

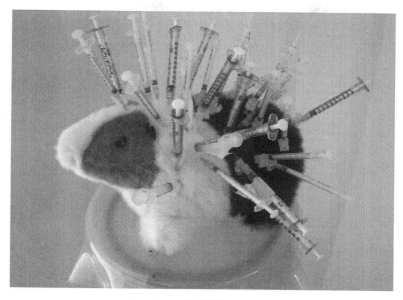

OUCH!!

The Q&A that followed was very different from the Q&A's at an annuity seminar. People here asked life and death questions about treatment options for their particular form of the thirty known non-Hodgkin's lymphoma categories.

I can't end this episode by saying, as I often do when leaving a seminar, "A good time was had by all." As we stepped out into the forty-eight-degree cold, each of us mulled over what we had heard. Some probably felt reassured; some probably felt their future was unclear—still in the hands of the gods and/or the expertise of their oncologist. And for those younger cancer victims survivors, there was the hope that new drugs would come down the pike just in time.

Errol and Gladys (our good friends) drove us to and from the seminar. Gladys recounted a joke:

Man approaches woman sitting on a bench at an assisted living facility. He asks if he can sit down with her. She gives her permission. She breaks the silence, "You look pale."

He replies. "I've been inside a lot."

She asks, "Why, the weather has been so nice. Where have you been?"

He answers, "I've been in prison."

She inquires, "Why, what did you do?"

He intones," I killed my wife."

She responds, "Oh, so you're single."

WHO WOULD DRIVE FORTY MILES
FOR A FREE WAFFLE?

You guessed it: only a free lunch junkie with severe withdrawal symptoms. It had been twenty-eight days since my last freebie, and I exhibited the common symptoms of depression, anxiety, and craving (for a free meal). The Christmas and New Year's holidays brought the seminar business to a screeching halt, and I was like an addict in need of a fix. That's why on January 12, 2011, I headed my car north at 7:15 a.m. for the twenty-mile trip to Lake Worth Gardens, an independent living facility, for a free breakfast featuring waffles "custom made by Chef Jerry of their Savory Expressions Dining Programs."

I love waffles, but I have to make a confession about my epicurean assessment of the food served at the various venues I visited in compiling these stories. I lost most of my sense of taste several years ago through a combination of an incompetent oral surgeon in Delray Beach and the ravages of old age. And as a side effect of my current round of chemotherapy, I've developed a metallic taste in my mouth. But this gustatory deficiency hasn't kept me from critiquing the quality of the food I've eaten at the myriad seminars I've attended, and why should it? Many of the art critics I've followed have bad taste, and they get paid big bucks to write reviews of what they allege passes as contemporary art.

But I digress; back to my story

8:05 a.m. Diane welcomes me. Tells me to sign in so I'll be eligible for drawing for prize. "What's the prize?" I inquire. Diane replies with a touch of pride in her voice, "A gift card for Carraba's Restaurant." Want to ask its value, but thought it better to keep on her good side till I see the whites of the waffles on my plate. Turns out I was smart to keep my mouth shut, because Diane then hands me a plastic pill box container as a souvenir.

Led to table with three other freeloaders and two guests who were interested in learning about the facility. Chef Jerry is hard at work making waffles for the forty or so residents and the handful of guests. One of the two waffle-griddle-making devices dies right in front of us. Waiter calls 911.

Join a long line of people seeking custom-made waffles. In the twenty-five minutes I get to exchange a few words with my tablemates. Ex-Brooklynites. One was a cabbie in Manhattan in the 1950s. Tells me a medallion now costs $800,000. I learn something every time I go freeloading.

8:30 a.m. Waffle arrives with bacon, syrup, butter, and berries. Delicious.

8:50 a.m. Diane asks who wants to go on tour—only those who go on tour are eligible for the prize drawing—I go on tour. There are only six others on tour, so have pretty good chance of winning— better than lottery.

Visit neat two-bedroom, two-bath apartment with nice view of Florida Turnpike. Costs $3,400 per month. Studios only $1,800. All with three meals. Wonder if all the kitchen equipment is in the same lousy shape as the waffle griddles. If so, meals could be a long affair.

End of tour. One woman says she'd like to get more information on a one-to-one basis. She's smart as a whip—she wins gift certificate for sure.

9:00 a.m. Go back into dining room. I have worked up quite an appetite on the tour. Jerry whips me up half a waffle with all the trimmings.

9:08 a.m. Back in car for twenty-mile return trip.

One highlight of this independent living facility is their extra-curricular activities. I finally found the right place for me. Every Monday at 1:15 p.m. there is a course on creative writing. Based on the reception I've so far received to this manuscript from the literary agents I've approached, this course is a *must*. If Lake Worth Gardens ever gets its second waffle iron fixed, I'll be ready to move in.

I GOT ANOTHER TWO BIRDS WITH ONE STONE

Business was still slow. It had been two weeks since my last free meal. Thank G_d for Merrill Lynch. Their invitation to a seminar at Morton's on "Wealth Structuring Issues and Strategies" sent my juices flowing. I was a little put off by the fact that the invite was only for "Cocktails and Hors D'Oeuvres." Pretty chintzy, especially since "This event is designated for investors with assets over $10 million." I might have to borrow $9 million or so from my friendly banker to qualify, but that should be easy—I'm as subprime as they get.

But a bigger hurdle loomed ahead. I saw in Judy's calendar book that we were having houseguests (Sylvia and Stan) that night. Yes, this is where the two birds get killed! I decided to invite Stan to join me at the seminar. He's interested in the stock market. He likes to drink. And I'm sure he'll feel indebted for the free food and booze and reciprocate with an invite for a night on the town for Judy and me.

We arrived at a little before 5 p.m. and parked in the empty lot across the street from Morton's. Stan was a little nervous about his first foray into the world of freeloading, which surprised me, because he is a practicing clinical psychologist. I assured him the sponsors wouldn't try to embarrass him into setting up a subsequent one-on-one meeting.

5:00 p.m. Enter private back room. Empty. Freezing. Take two chairs at one of four tables of eight. Waiter takes drink order. Stan hits them up for a Johnny Walker Black on the rocks. I order grapefruit juice. One of sponsors comes over to make nice. Stan thinks the guy really likes him because he asks so many personal questions. Couple from outside of Boston sit next to us. Tell us they are clients of Merrill and very happy.

Husband recounts how he built up a chain of twenty-three Dunkin' Donuts over a thirty-seven-year span. Sold out three years ago for megabucks. Real Horatio Alger with a Boston accent. His wife must have spent those thirty-seven years letting her nails grow. Her red-polished claws were curved like a cesta (the wicker basket a jai-alai player uses). Imagine she used these talons to scoop out the donut holes.

All tables fill up, but almost everyone present is existing client of Merrill's. The sponsors must have sent out several thousand expensively produced mailers seeking prospective clients, and they only snared two couples. Maybe they should have sprung for a full dinner instead of just drinks and hors d'oeuvres. Speaking of the latter, waiters pass plates of crab cakes (great), portabella cum cheese, tuna tartar (ugh), and the specialty of the house, filet mignon. Unfortunately the filet mignon consists of large bun containing a tiny sliver of steak—it is so thin can see light through it. Bob (one of the sponsors) catches me holding the sliver up to the light and gives me a strange look. He doesn't comment about this, but does tell me that it is strange that I have filled up a page of notes before the seminar has started.

Two men join our table and introduce themselves as "professional men from the area." Stan whispers, "Must be dentists." They do have great smiles.

Try to fill up on the hors d'oeuvres, but not an easy task. Stan gets in the spirit and orders a second drink. Lucky I'm driving.

5:40 p.m. Speaker spends next half hour talking about estate tax planning. He reports Republicans pushed through last-minute deal in

December 2010 offering never-before-seen opportunities for the very wealthy to avoid mega millions in estate taxes. I ask Stan to stand up and offer a toast to John Boehner et al, but he isn't drunk enough. Obama got a few thousand bucks for the unemployed as his half of the compromise. Rich or poor, it's better to be rich.

Highlight of the evening occurs during the Q&A session. Stan asks speaker if he forgot to mention an all-important caveat pertaining to one of the arcane points in his discourse. Speaker corrects Stan and continues his talk. The head honcho from the Merrill Group interrupts and says that Stan is right. I shine in Stan's reflected glory.

6:10 p.m. Another suit gives very brief opinion about the stock market.

6:15 p.m. Blonde real estate broker makes a belated entrance. Joins us. You wonder how I know she's a real estate broker. Well, it just happens that she lives in our community. We exchange hellos. She orders wine and hors d'ouevres and surveys the room. A cynic would say this recently widowed, heavily made-up, and over-dressed woman was here on the lookout for one of the male guests who met the $10 million asset requirement. But people who live in glass houses shouldn't throw stones.

6:30 p.m. Meeting over. No pressure from sponsors. Stan relaxes. We exit.

Stan told me he was still hungry. I decided to pull out all the stops and show him the time of his life. I had just received two coupons from Steak 'n Shake to commemorate my birthday. I treated Stan to their famous double cheeseburger with fries, and we sat in the car and savored our repast. (The coupons saved me $7.22, but from the satisfied look on Stan's face, I'm sure he thought I had spent a lot more.)

IF IT'S TUESDAY, THIS MUST BE MORTON'S

To commemorate my fiftieth free lunch/dinner seminar, I had a bowl of cornflakes at home with Judy for dinner. After a while the episodes seem to blur, one into another. Ruth's Chris, Morton's, Abe & Louie's, and Capital Grille are wonderful porterhouse pantheons for those who are devotees of prime beef, but to me they are more or less the same. And the presentations made by the major Wall Street investment firms that hold their seminars at these expensive steak sanctuaries were more or less carbon copies of one another (pontificate as if you have the answer to everyone's investment situation, ignore the lousy advice your firm gave prior to the market's crash, offer a free evaluation of any prospective client's portfolio, make nice and pass the wine). I don't blame the presenters. They seemed like a very nice group of people trying to make a living to support their families, and I don't for a moment doubt their sincerity, ability, and honesty.

I don't have the same warm and fuzzy feeling for some sponsors and salespeople who've pitched annuities to me. And it has nothing to do with the fact that these firms generally chose less-expensive restaurants for their seminars (Cheesecake Factory, Bonefish Grill, etc.) and usually omitted the salad or dessert or both.

If I were to generalize about the annuity presentations I've listened to, I'd say that they promise more than they deliver. At more than one seminar the presenter described one of his firm's products as "too good to be true." I tend to take them at their word on this one.

The third tier of seminars is made up of the "Do It Yourselfers." These companies provide breakfast or lunch in-house." Funeral chapels and cemeteries selling crypts and pre-planning packages, in addition to assisted living facilities, make up the sponsors of this kind of seminar. The type and quality of the food varies greatly, from heavily mayo-ed chunk-style tuna sandwiches to excellent tenderloin of beef. The big spenders in this category use Golden Corral and cheap Chinese restaurants (in Boca this is an oxymoron).

And the bottom of the barrel is represented by those seminars that offer light refreshments or charge a minimal amount for attendance. Doctors generally are found at the bottom of the barrel, and surprisingly enough their seminars usually garner large audiences, because every senior in Florida has one ailment or another. The surprising part is that any senior can get all the free advice he wants from any physician via Medicare. I guess they're just shopping for a second opinion. Speaking of second opinions, I've always found a lot of maids in attendance at seminars held by physicians. If you know why I wrote this last sentence, you can skip the following tale.

A man hurt his leg skiing one weekend. By the time he got home Saturday, the leg was very swollen and he was having difficulty walking, so he called his physician at his home. The doctor told him to soak it in hot water.

He tried soaking it in hot water, but the leg became more swollen and painful. His maid saw him limping and said, "I don't know, but I always thought it was better to use cold water, not hot, for swelling."

He tried switching to cold water, and the swelling rapidly subsided.

On Sunday afternoon he called his doctor again to complain. "Say, what kind of a doctor are you anyway? You told me to soak my leg in hot water, and it got worse. My maid told me to use cold water, and it got better."

"Really?" answered the doctor. "I don't understand it; my maid said to use hot water.

MY SWAN SONG WAS NOTHING TO SING ABOUT

February 11, 2011 will go down in history (infamy?) as the day I attended my last free lunch seminar. I reached my goal of attending fifty such meetings in just ten months and Mr. Guinness is considering including my feat in the next edition of his "Book of World Records." I quaffed a pint of ale to celebrate the occasion

The reason for the downbeat title to this episode had nothing to do with a swan, but with a bird of a different feather, a chicken. My host for this momentous occasion, a retirement life community, served up a less than satisfying slab of chicken for my final luncheon.

I'm certainly the last person in Boca Raton who should be looking a gift horse in the mouth, but I think I just ate one. I did not let this gastronomic deficiency cast a pall on such an historic day. Here's a recap of an otherwise very interesting two and a half hour adventure.

10:30 a.m. Sign in and have nametag slapped on my shirt for the final time. Enter large meeting room and am surprised to find a large crowd of fifty some odd, and some not so odd, seniors sitting facing a large projection screen. Help myself to coffee and a mini Danish. In front of the room is a large wooden six-sided star on the left complimented by a similar sized cross on the right.

Speaker is an ex social worker from Rochester who found her calling working for this consortium of twenty-three retirement communities in eight states. Unlike all the other senior communities have visited this one combines the three stages or residences (independent living, assisted living and nursing care) into one package deal. You put up in advance (non-refundable) from $100,000 to $283,000 (1BR to 3 BR) for housing in their independent living section.

Man in audience raises his hand and says he's never heard of such a large lump-sum payment and he's traveled the circuit. Speaker doesn't miss a beat. Says, "Ours is not for everyone. We want you to check around and find the right place for you. But, ask any of the residents of this facility (a group of whom were in the room to serve as guides) and they'll tell you they love it here.

Well I couldn't care less whether it's a good idea or not — I'm here for a free lunch — and as it turned out so were some of the people with whom I broke bread. But in my excitement I've gotten ahead of myself.

Learn the conglomerate is a non-profit organization. All profits reinvested. Seems strange.

Movie extols virtue of facility.

11:15 a.m. Tour facility and view 2BR 2B model apartment led by resident who loves the place. 12:00 p.m. Take assigned seat at cramped table for seven, one of whom is a resident who also loves the place. She and husband came from Century Village nine months ago and they love it.

Napkin is in glass and can't figure out whether mine is on my right or left. I ask question.

Opinion is divided. Take napkin on my right.

Tablemate on left says he lives in Century Village and loves it. "Why did you come?" I inquire, looking to cause a little trouble. He takes up my gauntlet and replies with a broad smile on his face "For the free lunch and I also wanted to get out of the house." Tells us he's recently widowed, lonely and hates cooking for himself.

His table neighbor also lives in Century Village.

Resident asks me where I live. "Century Village," I respond, not wanting to make waves so far from the beach. "Which one?" she inquires. "Boca," I reply and she nods in acknowledgement. We're all joined at the hip.

Salad (very green), ice in iced tea has completely melted (global warming hits Boca) followed by sub-par chicken and very tasty chocolate layer cake.

Speaker asks us to fill in info card with name and address and add whether we want to have a follow up meeting. About to throw my card away when she adds that everyone who hands in a card will get a parting gift. Hand my card in. Get a lime green bag with the name of the Senior Living Facility emblazoned on it. Fitting end to my career.

I got back in the car with a smile on my face and a tear in my heart. I know I'll miss the free food, the many interesting people I've met –– even the slick, hard-selling promoters who wanted to separate me from some of my hard earned cash.

Bon appétit.

SEMINAR SCENES

(from top left clockwise) 1. My very first free lunch at The Cheesecake Factory.
2. "All gone" at The Marriott. 3. A $6.99 lunch at Red Lobster. 4. To die from at
Toojay's. 5. A box lunch seminar at the JCC.

SEMINAR SCENES

(from top left clockwise) 1. Café Boulud in Palm Beach 2. Men's Room Mizner style 3. Pancake breakfast at a Retirement Facility 4. Two lousy mini-Danish is all I got at a surgeon's seminar. 5. The Holy Grail — a porterhouse at Ruth's Chris 6. A packed house at Brook's.

Made in the USA
Lexington, KY
18 July 2013